Presented To:

_____

From:

_____

Date:

_____

The Single Parent's Guide to Love, Dating, and Relationships

Shae Cooke

Finding love in all the right places

© Copyright 2011–Shae Cooke

All rights reserved. This book is protected by the copyright laws of the United States of America. This book may not be copied or reprinted for commercial gain or profit. The use of short quotations or occasional page copying for personal or group study is permitted and encouraged. Permission will be granted upon request. Unless otherwise identified, Scripture quotations are taken from the New King James Version. Copyright © 1982 by Thomas Nelson, Inc. Used by permission. All rights reserved. Please note that Destiny Image's publishing style capitalizes certain pronouns in Scripture that refer to the Father, Son, and Holy Spirit, and may differ from some publishers' styles. Take note that the name satan and related names are not capitalized. We choose not to acknowledge him, even to the point of violating grammatical rules.

DESTINY IMAGE® PUBLISHERS, INC.

P.O. Box 310, Shippensburg, PA 17257-0310

"Speaking to the Purposes of God for This Generation and for the Generations to Come."

This book and all other Destiny Image, Revival Press, MercyPlace, Fresh Bread, Destiny Image Fiction, and Treasure House books are available at Christian bookstores and distributors worldwide.

For a U.S. bookstore nearest you, call 1-800-722-6774.

For more information on foreign distributors, call 717-532-3040.

Reach us on the Internet: www.destinyimage.com.

ISBN 13 TP: 978-0-7684-3663-1

ISBN 13 HC: 978-0-7684-3664-8

ISBN 13 LP: 978-0-7684-3665-5

ISBN 13 Ebook: 978-0-7684-9033-6

For Worldwide Distribution, Printed in the U.S.A.

1 2 3 4 5 6 7 8 9 10 11 / 13 12 11

Dedication

I dedicate this book to the world's greatest champions, you, the single parent, and your children, and pray it opens wide the eyes of your heart to trust the miracle of love again.

Acknowledgments

The birth of this guidebook series emerged from the compassionate heart of Jonathan Nori of Destiny Image Publishing, who saw the many challenges, heartbreaks, and wrestlings of the solo parent. Without Jon's God-inspired vision and invitation to me to write from the heart, these books would not have happened. Thank you, Jonathan, for your heart of gold, and to the Destiny powers, support staff, and single-parent Destiny employees who provided feedback and joined us in this project.

To DS, my beloved precious son, who has provided me with so much insight, and has taught me that parenting is as much for me as it is for him: Son, your wisdom amazes me, and you really rock! Thank you for your sacrifices, sweet one.

To my son's father: No hard feelings. What happened between us has taught me a huge lesson in forgiveness, and for that, I am eternally grateful. We have an incredible son, who deep down inside desires the best for both of us, and the best of both of us!

To my foster parents (both sets): Father and Mother B, and to Maman and Papa, who modeled unconditional love, accepting me for who I was, and for tenaciously holding on, even through my tumultuous teen years.

To my mother, whose love shone even through her own nightmarish life, and carried me through every transition: I am certain you petitioned God on my behalf to ensure the best possible outcomes for my life.

To my Auntie Etta: You modeled singleness in the most perfect way.

To my brothers and sisters who continue to support and champion me in my endeavors and love-life: You inspire me to go on!

To the many anonymous parents who openly shared their hearts for this book: Thank you.

To my Father.

Epigraph

Where there is great love there are always miracles.
     WILLA CATHER (1873–1947)
     Pulitzer Prizewinning author

Contents

INTRODUCTION 13

PART ONE
Finding The Real You For The Perfect Person........... 15

CHAPTER ONE
Courage to Jump Into Shark-Infested Waters 17
Overcoming the Fear of Dating

CHAPTER TWO
Sometimes You Can Get a Splinter
Even Sliding Down a Rainbow 37
Evaluating Your Regrets

CHAPTER THREE
Wake Up and Smell the Double Mocha Latte!......... 55
Creating More Favorable Heart Conditions

CHAPTER FOUR
One Doesn't Have to Be the Loneliest Number 77
How to Be Singularly Spectacular

PART TWO
Finding The Perfect Person For The Real You........... 97

CHAPTER FIVE
I Beg Your Pardon, I Never Promised You a Rose Garden... 99
Avoiding Regrets in Your Search for Love

CHAPTER SIX
You Can't Date or Remarry. Not Never!
...And You Shouldn't Have...Sex?..........................119
Your Children, Your Dating, and You

CHAPTER SEVEN
Do Flowers in Spring Say, "Not Yet"?................. 133
How to See, Find, and Fit the Right Person Into Your Life

CHAPTER EIGHT
Bad Boys, Bad Girls—Whatcha Gonna Do? 155
(Whatcha Gonna Do When They Come for You?)

CHAPTER NINE
Honey, I've Got Your Number...................... 181
How to Break Up or Make Up Well

CHAPTER TEN
Try Again, Draw a Long Breath, and Believe.......... 197
Take Your Relationship to Extraordinary Heights

SUMMARY 219

Introduction

It should come as no surprise that we learn from our mistakes and regrets, especially when they involve say, eight or nine failed romances, two marriages, and many bungled attempts at love! However, a less painful way for us to learn—which causes less upset to our children—is from other people's emotional chaos and fumbles, their learning journeys and successes through them—and it doesn't hurt one iota to laugh about a few things. The good news is, I have succeeded in love, and I want to encourage you, it is worth the wait.

Thus, at my expense and for the benefit of the 12.9[1] million single moms and dads in America and the millions more in Canada and around the world who cannot afford more heartbreak—and of course, for the benefit of the casualties of loss, our sons and daughters—I've sought my own heart, challenges, and victories, and the experiences and consensuses of other single moms and dads who have experienced their own unique heartbreaks and losses while navigating love, to provide you with the best possible real world encouragement, helps, and compass points on what could be an incredible journey.

Most parents agreed that they needed help with the unloading of some heavy emotional baggage before moving on and even in hoping for a successful remarriage outcome, so we start there, getting you healed up and s-t-r-e-t-c-h-e-d to believe the very best person for you and for your family, so that you can help your children believe the same. My purpose in the first few chapters is to take you on a journey of healing and self growth for its own value to you and your children, today. You don't need to suffer from the past or the present anymore. Such healing will naturally magnetize your appeal, beautify you from the inside out, so that people will want in, right into the depths of who you are! It also puts you on the love track, to defining, attracting, and finding the right person for you and your family. Moreover, it helps you stick to your guns when it comes to never settling for less than you and your children deserve!

Comedian Robin Williams said: "You're only given a little spark of madness. You mustn't lose it." I can assure you, you'll find a few of those sparks in this guide. I'm so glad you've picked up this copy, and pray it fills you with courage, confidence, and fortitude to wholeheartedly love and trust again.

Yours in Love,
SHAE COOKE

Endnote

1. U.S. Census Bureau, Single-Parent Households Show Little Variation Since 1994, released March 27, 2007. Available at http://www.census.gov/newsroom/releases/archives/families_households/cb07-46.html.

PART ONE

Finding The Real You
For The Perfect Person

Chapter One

Courage to Jump Into Shark-Infested Waters

Overcoming the Fear of Dating

Where the fin of the shark cuts like a black chip out of the water...

—from "Song of Myself"
by WALT WHITMAN

Most people live in fear of sharks, believing them to be vicious, flesh-eating killing machines. *Jaws*, the 1975 blockbuster movie, didn't help. The decision not to swim in shark-infested waters is usually an "I want to live" reflex. This "I don't wanna be shark bait" feeling is also common among single parents reentering the waters of dating; the thrashing, the circling, the gnashing—it is all just a little too unsettling and confusing at times. It helps to know though that sharks aren't always as brave or mean as we think, nor are they sure of what they want, either. If they could figure us out, they probably would. We're going to try to fix that!

Many years ago as a teen, while swimming in the ocean on Cape Cod (I was summering there with my foster parents), a sand shark, dead and belly up, floated past. I freaked and splashed to shore for my life. A shark was a shark, and all sharks—dead or alive—were evil. I couldn't stop thinking, *what if?* What if the shark had been alive...if there were others about...had it chomped off my leg...my torso...yikes! Anticipating the worst, like being the butt of "Eileen Tu Oneside" jokes for the rest of my life, not even my big toe touched the water for the rest of the holiday. I missed out on gobs of fun, as a result.

Had I known the truth about sharks—that dead they are harmless, and alive most are not such threats after all, I might have searched them out, or, even have had the courage to swim with, touch, or even hug one or two, as Rob Stewart, a 28-year-old biologist from Canada, does. Stewart loved sharks as a child, researching and discovering them as awesome ocean creatures and later dedicating his career working to understand and save them. He worked to gain their trust and "to prove that it won't cost you an arm and a leg to get to know them—fearsome teeth and all."[1]

Stewart calmly enters waters all over the world with only his undersea camera to get up close and downright personal with the these ocean predators, to challenge our fears. Most shark bites he explains as "shark mistakes."

Further, that when the shark discovers that it has something in its jaws it doesn't want, and it lets go—hence, why most people only lose a limb or a chunk of flesh in a shark attack. (Some mistake!)[2]

> "Come to the edge," he said.
> They said, "We are afraid."
> "Come to the edge," he said.
> They came.
> He pushed them...
> And they flew.
> —CHRISTOPHER LOGUE[3]

I was terrified at the prospect of my first post-breakup date, a blind date, with Ray the dentist,[4] a wonderful guy; crazy wealthy with two practices, and a Good Samaritan at that. He frequently gave of his time and resources in third world countries with Doctors Without Borders. He owned a crazy large penthouse at English Bay, the hottest place to live in Vancouver; drove a Lamborghini, *and,* miracles of miracles, *deeply* desired marriage—was ready to buy an estate in the burbs, settle down with the right person. Children welcome. Free dentistry and orthodontics for life. Ray the Dentist was a single mother's dream; it should have thrilled me to meet him, at the very least because eight-year-old DS[5] would need braces within a few years, but my automatic response was to view him as a threat—*The man will hurt me. He's doctor death. He will either take a chunk out of me or swallow me whole. A shark is a shark, a man is a man, a dentist is a torturer*—the annoying Energizer Bunny® of my imaginations played on and on and on. The poor guy didn't have a chance. I stood him up.

~~Twice.~~ Five times.

Ray the Dentist was tenacious, and very patient, I'll give him that!

We are taught our whole life to fear sharks as monsters, and this conditioning keeps us out of the water. Recall, the biologist sought the truth, and the truth *motivated him* into the shark-infested waters. Think about it. He learned as a child through knowledge that sharks are beautiful creatures, and he set out on a journey that would not only transform his own life but also change the way people view the sharks, not as fearful things to destroy but as vital treasures to care for and preserve.

Had I known the truth about men—that all were not sharks; had I debunked the lie that all marriages fail, had I discovered that most dentists aren't hell-bent on causing pain, had I known the truth about myself, that I was a catch, perhaps I would not have eyed him with such wariness, and who knows? He could have been my treasure! Ray did meet and fall in love with a woman, a single mother, only a month after I stood him up, and they married within 90 days. Ironically, her name was "Peg," but all limbs were intact!

 CATCH THE DRIFT: What or who are the sharks in your life? Are your fears unfounded, or do you have reasons why you fear them?

On the Road to Healthy Perceptions

Because I had been hurt more than once in relationships, I viewed romantic prospects with suspicion, expecting betrayal, and listening to that voice that told me to expect guys to hurt me in some way. My avoidance was the byproduct of conditioning reflex—self-programmed self-abasement, and of resultant fear based on the "what ifs" of both past and future. Had my perceptions been healthy, I likely would have stayed in the present and been busier in the dating arena than a one-legged River Dancer, since the conditions of our present help to shape the future. *Webster's Dictionary* describes fear as "expectation with alarm." Ding! Ding! Ding! I expected and imagined the worst, and lost out on a potentially great relationship as a result.

When I did finally cough up the courage to date, if a love interest did not deliver as I imagined, I would push him toward it as a test, and usually, he'd run! Then of course, I'd wonder why, or vow that all men were alike, or that something was wrong with me, and wallow in self-pity. Acting unlovable, I lashed out at all those who dared love me—family, friends, the dog. Only when I finally faced the truth that I had worth and beauty, only when I chose not to listen to the negative inward chatter and instead chose to believe that I was deserving of love, not a burden, not *"down girl"* bad, could I live as a lovely and lovable fearless person, and view others with a more forgiving and trusting eye.

Fears That Work for Us

Understandably, our fears tend to dominate our lives, especially in the first few months or so following a loss or breakup, when we are still so tender and feeling vulnerable. No way do we want our children to experience another loss or put them through another breakup, nor do we want to go through it again. These are protective fears that for a time work for us, giving us time to adjust, heal, and get our family and lives back together again; but they usually disappear when true danger is past. This "good" fear, if you can call it that, causes us to stay on land when the sea is rough, or to run for cover in a lightning storm. This fear is working for us, but it usually subsides when the threat subsides.

Fears That Work Against Us

There are fears, however, that work against us; they last, perpetuate, enslave, or imprison. Such fears took hold of me in potentially unhealthy and self-defeating ways.

I feared I might not ever find someone to love. So I didn't bother to look. That if I did find someone, he would hurt my son. So I avoided men. I feared someone's love running out for me. So I turned down second dates. That I would grow old alone. So I let myself go. I feared I was ugly. So I withdrew socially. That I might never feel whole again. So I stopped dreaming. I feared meeting a wolf in sheep's clothing. So I stopped trusting. That I would repeat mistakes. So I stopped trying. I feared settling for someone just because I wanted to feel loved again, not because I was in love. So I stopped feeling. That I would crumble again. So I stopped living. I feared how my son would react to a stepfather. So I let him for a time, call the shots regarding my dating. That I would be too tired and jaded to be open to love again. So I resolved to become a romantic recluse. And I even feared my fears; that they would hold me back from all the good I knew both my son and I deserved.

Until I could deal with my plethora of fears, I found healing of the pains of the past difficult, forgiving my ex difficult, making right decisions, settling my son and I into a new life, believing in a hopeful future, all difficult. My fears led to confusion about my priorities, about my worth and abilities as a single mother, as a woman, as a shoe shopper, as a human being! Oy. You don't want to be confused! Oh my gosh, it was rough to know what to do, especially with all the incoming conflicting comments, advice and counseling from well-meaning (and not so well-meaning) friends, family members, counselors, and from a few so-called "experts" in books, articles, and on different blogs.

My friend Marie wanted to set me up with a date right away. "You shouldn't be alone," she said over my "I vant to be alone" objections. An online girlfriend (whom I've never met) wanted me to exact revenge against my ex. "Are you *really* going to let him get away with what he did?" An advice expert suggested I settle for an eternally single life. The most difficult comments were from those who'd say, "I'm glad you broke up, you deserved better," or, "I never liked him/trusted him in the first place." Grrr...and I'm like, "Well, why didn't you tell me that while I was dating him already!"

Fear of rejection, fear of being forgotten, fear of being unloved—most people have these fears. According to Max Lucado in his book *Fearless: Imagine Your Life Without Fear,* we fear that we don't matter, we fear nothingness, insignificance, evaporation.[6] Evaporation! How many times I felt I did not even exist! In truth, I did not; the confident, self-assured, good-natured woman went *poof!*

> CATCH THE DRIFT: What are you afraid of? Does it work for you, or against you? What is it costing you?

Trauma Can Resurrect Old Fears

The "tomorrow is another day" Scarlett O'Hara escape approach just didn't cut it. My fears did not disappear when I ignored them, put them off, pushed them aside; the unhealthy ones demanded my attention, and it took great effort at times to expose them, so that I could heal and thrive in my new life and help my son to mend. Imagining life without these fears was a seemingly impossible task.

The trauma of our family breakup reactivated and inflamed some self-beliefs that I'd both knowingly and unknowingly held onto for many years. For instance, as a foster child moved about from home to home and school to school, I worried that I would not be accepted. My breakup made this belief all the worse, and I feared the future, believing there was no way anyone could ever love me. This fear, for a time, ran the show. Who would ever want a relationship with me? Will I be sent away again? The unknown overwhelmed me.

How to Allay Fear

The fact is, nobody knows for certain what will happen in the next second, the next week, or the next year. It is a simple fact of being human. Nor can we truly control the future. Granted, we can live our lives in such a way that will improve our opportunities for a favorable outcome, but at the very least, this requires noticing our fears, rising from them, and believing in a great future; and then taking the necessary steps to get there. The good news is, we *can* control ourselves and we can *plan*, and this can help to alleviate many fears. Faith in God also helped me. When I favorably shaped my present, including in it a Higher Power who had my best interests at heart, then confusion fled and I arrived at a juncture of determining I wanted love again, that my future could be better than it had been. I took the road that would move me closer to those goals.

Following are a few of many of the steps that I took to help alleviate or allay my fears of relationship and commitment:

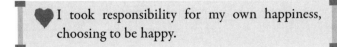
I took responsibility for my own happiness, choosing to be happy.

- I realized that there are no guarantees that any relationship will last. As it had in the past, something could happen today...tomorrow...next year to radically change things. Thus, I resolved to live a wonderful life by loving in whatever moment presented itself.

- I created a list of my fears concerning dating and commitment. Labeling what I was feeling inside helped alleviate some confusion. Many of my fears had to do with my son and his happiness and future. Seeing them on paper, in some instances, sparked memories that revealed their underlying causes. Some root causes were the result of one situation. Others were the result of present conditions. Thus, I set to work to find resolution or closure to the regrets, hurts, and conditions that created those fears. Please note, if your fears are causing anxiety, depression, or suicidal thoughts, get counseling, see a rabbi or pastor, or contact a doctor for help.

- I shared my fears with my love interest and asked him for his support and help through the process of dealing with them. In the absence of a partner, do consider counseling. A professional can help tailor a plan unique to the root of your fears.

- I resolved to say "yes" to my healthy yearnings, and vowed to stop depriving myself of happiness.

> ♥ I developed an attitude of gratitude, and daily thought about the things I was grateful for. It was amazing how transformational and empowering it was.
>
> ♥ I drew closer to God, who knows me better than I know myself!

"Nothing in life is to be feared, it is only to be understood. Now is the time to understand more, so that we may fear less."
—Nobel Prize recipient MARIE CURIE
(1867–1934)[7]

Fear was my clue that change needed to happen, and looking back, I'm grateful for it because it caused me to fear less about dating in that it heightened awareness of my low self-esteem, regrets, and trust problems, propelling me to search for true answers. Consequently, my fears at the very least helped me understand myself better, and my discoveries acted as gateways to conquer other fears, even closing the doors on some. In overcoming my fear of acceptance, for instance, I was able to move from baby steps to larger steps and I gained confidence in my lovability! Trust me. If you feel lovable, you'll be huggable, and everyone will want to come and squeeze you, for the right reasons! Well, perhaps the odd one for the wrong reasons. That's in another chapter.

The Root of Most Fear

Lies are at the root of most fears. Find the lie, discover the truth, and in most cases, the fear vanishes, or at least, courage will be on your radar. Unearth the truth, and you can face or alleviate the fear, giving you greater clarity for the choices you have to make.

> CATCH THE DRIFT: Evaluate your self-talk the next time you meet someone of interest, that gabby voice inside your head. What is it saying? Is it telling you that you failed before and likely will again? Is it telling you that you will never get over your grief? Is it saying, "He won't like me"? "She'll hurt me"? That voice is out to sabotage your happiness! Take the time to stop, listen, and filter what you "hear" before your first or next date, separating the truth from the lies, aborting the lies altogether. As you recognize the truth, you will understand your danger zones and become aware of self-defeating habits, and healthier behaviors should follow.

Hurtful or fearful memories of a soured relationship, if we don't take care of them properly and find closure, will sabotage the present. We'll always be treading water feeling like bait. The past blends into the present and every "land-ho" possibility for a radically better future presents as a mirage because we cannot comprehend the past *not* blending into tomorrow as well. To choose to allow lies to distort our dream of finding the right person, or allow a fear to render us unable to pursue what we desire, is to choose to be victimized by it. If we are not careful, we may develop a victim mindset, one that automatically and without forethought can unfavorably impact our behavior or action.

The Power of Faith

> "Take the first step in faith. You don't have to see the whole staircase, just take the first step."
> —Dr. Martin Luther King Jr.[8]

How I love Dr. King's wisdom. Just take the first step in faith. I shudder to think how color-minded this world would be had this heroic leader not taken those brave first steps in the advancement of civil rights in the United States and around the world. His efforts, every step he took, advanced the cause; led him to that memorable 1963 march on Washington to deliver his "I Have a Dream" speech, where he expanded American values to include the vision of a color-blind society.[9] What many do not realize is that in his last years, he also focused his efforts on ending poverty and the Vietnam War. Faith filled King with courage to step into dangerous waters of opposition.

> CATCH THE DRIFT: This might be a good time to take stock of your beliefs. What do you believe in? In whom do you believe? What is your greatest hope? What is your greatest fear? How is it an obstacle, or is it? How great is your faith?

Searching for a new love requires a step of faith. Faith is so much more rational, powerful, and full of possibilities and empowerment than fear, which is irrational at the best of times. Faith, once you have committed to it, empowers you to choose the manner in which you respond to your fears. Have faith that you will know the joy of a true love relationship, that your future is bright with promise. Believe that you are lovable, beautiful, handsome, a treasure deserving of a bright future. Choose to work through your fears, to discover the truth. No book, no human person, can make you fearless or completely alleviate your fears; only you can choose to replace fear with faith-filled hope. Faith came to me when I changed my attitude, when I looked back on my childhood and realized that I had come through (relatively) unscathed. When I realized I had survived another day alone. When I realized many challenges of the past were successfully overcome. In the glow of the faith in my Higher Power, the Lord Jesus Christ ever ready to help me, who had always been there, I gained confidence to overcome my fears of being unloved and unlovable, my fears of being hurt again, and even the fear of being alone should the love of my life never come along. Negative self-talk goes *poof* when you have faith, and especially when you believe in someone bigger than anything out there that can bring you harm. Those two nuggets alone can have the power to transform your reality.

The Only Real Fear to Fear

"The only thing we have to fear is fear itself," said President Franklin D. Roosevelt in his inaugural address during the Depression.[10] Respectfully, I disagree, in the context I've noted. Fear can *clue us in* to a problem, and can also change us in a good way, if we seek to overcome it. A fearful past relationship experience or even the fear of another loss can make us wiser, stronger, and more knowledgeable, transforming the Eileen Tu Onesides in all of us, if we choose to turn it over for the good.

Turning the tide a little here, what we should fear is that of becoming embittered and hateful, intolerant and unforgiving of others and of ourselves. Nobody wants to date Jaws! Such behavior ignites fear and signals peril. If you want people to swim with you, treat you right, you have to prove that it won't cost them an arm or a leg to know you. It won't, right?

If you are to ever believe that when they are dead, love prospects are harmless, and when they are alive, most are not such threats after all; if you are to have the courage to hop into the dating pool, then you must uncover the lies and *discover the truth*, and it will truly free you to love again and take that first faith-filled step. Du-doo. Du-doo. Du-doo. Du-doo....

Below the Surface

Your answers to these questions may change as you go through the process of healing and discovery, and into relationship, perhaps even as you read through this book in retrospection. Thus, you'll find these questions in each chapter. Record and date your answers. Review later, and see what, if anything, has changed.

Date: _____

Are my children OK?
___
___
___

What are their fears?
___
___
___

What do they need?
___
___
___

Who or what is my ultimate concern right now?
___
___

Courage to Jump Into Shark-Infested Waters

What has happened to me?

What is happening to me?

What's next?

What do I really want?

Why am I worried?

What am I most afraid of?

What is deep down inside of me that I haven't brought forth yet?

What do I have to offer?

What truths or lies have shaped my perceptions of me?

How faithful am I to my yearnings?

What sacrifices have I made?

Who has sacrificed for me?
_____
_____
_____

What am I grateful for?
_____
_____
_____

Who can I reach out to?
_____
_____
_____

Who is the top person in my support network?
_____
_____
_____

Who do I need to forgive?
_____
_____
_____

Endnotes

1. BLOG: "Life in the Fast Lane" Article title: 7 Incredible and Bizarre Underwater Inventions and Feats, appearing

June 5, 2008, accessed May 28, 2010. Blog belonging to Fast Lane Transport, Ltd., Edmonton, Alberta. Article by Deborah Petersen. And the movie trailer for "Sharkwater" www.sharkwater.com, accessed and viewed May 28, 2010.

2. *Ibid.*
3. Nigel Rees, *Cassel's Companion to Quotations* (London: Sterling Publishing Co., 1997), p. 359.
4. Name changed for privacy.
5. DS is for Dear Son, the name I give my son for reasons of his privacy.
6. Max Lucado, *Fearless: Imagine Your Life Without Fear* (Nashville, TN: Thomas Nelson Publishers, 2009), chapter 2.
7. Marie Curie, quoted at http://thinkexist.com/quotation/ nothing_in_life_is_to_be_feared-it_is_only_to_be/145431 .html.
8. Martin Luther King Jr., quoted at http://www.great-quotes .com/quote/898888.
9. Martin Luther King Jr., "I Have a Dream," speech given on the steps of the Lincoln Memorial, Washington, DC, August 28, 1963.
10. Franklin D. Roosevelt, Inaugural Address, March 4, 1933, as published in Samuel Rosenman, ed., *The Public Papers of Franklin D. Roosevelt, Volume Two: The Year of Crisis, 1933* (New York: Random House, 1938), 11-16. Available at http://historymatters.gmu.edu/d/5057/.

Chapter Two

Sometimes You Can Get a Splinter Even Sliding Down a Rainbow[1]

Evaluating Your Regrets

> "It's not that easy bein' green...
> Having to spend each day the color of the leaves
> when I think it could be nicer
> being red or yellow or gold
> or something much more colorful like that.
> It's not easy bein' green.
> It seems you blend in with so
> many other ordinary things.
> And people tend to pass you over
> 'cause you're not standing out like
> flashy sparkles in the water...."
> —"Bein' Green," by Joe Raposo for Sesame Street[2]

Single parents tend to have the greater share of life's regrets because of taking on the added heartbreaks and burdens that our children have, but unless we can break through especially the deep, intense, painful regrets in healthy ways now, while we are still single, we will be bringing a whole lot of unwelcome baggage into a future relationship and at best, that relationship will be like licking honey off a thorn.[3]

My sudden breakup in the spring of 2004 with Nathan[4] toppled my life and hurled me into a frothing and fierce backwash of burdensome regrets that caused emotional chaos in my heart concerning the future. Some nights I tried to erase the whole relationship from memory, and certain days I wondered how I would ever manage on my own. And how would our child fare through all this? Become another statistic? Desires, dreams, and determination fizzled, and I lost faith for what I'd hoped for my whole life: to be the best wife, to have the husband of my dreams, to provide my children with the best father, while growing up in the most loving buttercup- and dandelion-filled home.

I had many questions: Why did it happen, and the way it did? Why did I choose him? What was wrong with me? Why did the relationship bomb? Was I destined to repeat the mistakes of my parents? I made the choice to be with him with good intention (although I was on the rebound and not ready for a relationship), for better or for worse; and tried so hard to make things work. I wanted it to work. Our son, DS—only eight—he *needed* this to work, which is the first of two reasons why I overstayed my welcome.

When You Wish You Wasn't But You Is

Enter No Man's Land, and eventually I'm wondering what life would have been like had I married anyone I'd ever dated or had a crush on, good or bad. Of course, I imagined my precious DS with me in those lives.

I recall reading about an old flame's latest movie and the status of his love life, and wondering how things would have turned out had things become serious with us. I met Jim Carrey (the hilarious star of *Batman Forever; The Mask; Ace Ventura: Pet Detective; Dumb and Dumber; Bruce Almighty; Liar Liar; Me, Myself & Irene,* and other movies) around 1979 or 1980 while we were both at challenging life junctures, in states certainly of introspection, and wondering when things would truly break for us.[5] (This is usually when people tend to be at their most vulnerable and make the most relationship mistakes.)

Jimmy, in his late teens, and about two years younger than me, had been performing as the headliner at a comedy restaurant/club in downtown Montreal where my sister worked as a bartender, and where I often hung out in the months after a devastating breakup with an older man who I thought was the love of my life. This heartbreak followed on the heels of my mother's sudden death in a fire. Thus, I was dealt a double whammy. Whether my time at Maxwells was to be in the comforting presence of my sweet big sister, just for laughs, or to drown my sorrows, I am uncertain, but it was a difficult inward time for me of mourning, sadness, confused whys, and lack of direction.

Leaving the Prince, Loving the Frog

I had arrived early before his set, and my sister introduced us. He wasn't my type—skinny, young, pimple-faced, awkward, and with a goofy chipped tooth, but the magnetic force of our challenges, our grasps toward the uncertain, and our similar pasts clasped us together almost instantly, and we spent his remaining time in Montreal and all of our free time together, in his words, as "two peas in a pod." Jimmy's dream was to pull his family out of poverty and into a better life, and in fact, he had a vision, a mission, and a goal to get it, and proved it by pulling out a check for $10 million[6] made out to himself.

It is hard to think of Jimmy as anything but outwardly spastic, but as rip-roaringly hilarious as he was, he, like me, was an inward-pondering soul. Certainly, we seemed cut from the same stalk, having both lived our childhoods on the wrong side of the tracks; sharing the desire to make something of ourselves to help our loved ones, needing affirmation and love and humor in our lives, and in a stage of wondering when true breakthrough would come.

"It's not easy bein' green...,"[7] crooned Jimmy one day as we shared a Coke at a coffeeshop counter. Surprisingly, he metamorphosed into adorable Kermit the Frog, bulging his eyes into ping-pongs, thinning his lips, and smiling outrageously wider than his ears. Goading me into the role of Miss Piggy (the prima donna diva pig bent on bagging Kermit for a husband)—and in full view of all the diners—we finished singing "Bein' Green" together.

Spending time with Jimmy was like dating a hundred men all at once. He could rubberize himself into Elvis, Jack Nicholson, Dick Van Dyke, John Wayne, and a hundred more characters at least—human and cartoon—nailing every tic, inflection, and nuance of their personalities. He believed that his big break would come on the Johnny Carson show, as he said that the then-popular late-night talk show host loved comedians who could impersonate him well, and frequently gave those ones, such as he had done for Rich Little (another Canadian) their big breaks on his show. One time, Jimmy disappeared into the sweet character of Jimmy Stewart as Elwood P. Dowd in the movie *Harvey* and did not reappear for hours, and I was in h-e-a-v-e-n. "Miss Kelly, perhaps you'd like this flower...I seem to have misplaced my buttonhole." I melted!

Imagine having that kind of talent and ability to drift into different personas as fluidly and as at will as a turtle pops its head out of a shell! When he did resurface, I pleaded for him to slip back into character! (Would that all exes had that ability!) Once, though, he transformed into Cher, and I was like outta there, *yikes* thank-you-very-much! "I want Jimmy back, *now!*" I pleaded.

> Imagine having that kind of talent and ability to drift into different personas as fluidly and as at will as a turtle pops its head out of a shell! When he did resurface, I pleaded for him to slip back into character!

One morning, Jimmy asked for ice, dumped the entire bucket in the sink with water, and dunked his face into it. This was a daily ritual which he claimed kept his face "pliable." He would practice different mugs in the mirror or ask me what I thought of this impression or that joke, and I'd be on the floor, sides splitting. He was playful, too—and we roughed and tumbled together as children do. In hindsight, we *were* children!

Our brief "romance" ended as suddenly as it began, before he soared into superstardom, with Jimmy heading back to Ontario. The relationship never grew into the commitment phase, and we lost touch. The one person he could not impersonate was my prince, or, perhaps my kisses just didn't work. Today I am grateful, and don't even regret missing out on the lifestyle of the rich and famous, for I doubt our relationship would have lasted in Divorce Central, otherwise known as Hollywood; and I don't know that I could have survived his antics! Moreover, and most importantly, Jimmy had a life-long hope of worldly success and acceptance that I did not share, and that I don't believe factored in true commitment toward any one person.

Et moi? To this day, I do not know if I fell in love with him (in Miss Piggy fashion, of course), or with one of his characters, but I do know that he gave me the gift of knowing what I did not want—a tailless fly-eating amphibian for a husband, for starters! Seriously, I preferred to have someone in my life interested in pursuing bliss with *me,* and not with the world. (If I remember right, the divine porcine desired both!)

Our paths crossed briefly a few years later in Vancouver, British Columbia, where I had relocated in 1980. My new husband, Phil,[8] and I were walking onto a ferry that would take us over to Vancouver Island for a school reunion. Disembarking passengers headed down the gangway toward us, and among them was Jimmy, with a full entourage—and a woman on his arm. I had not followed his career and had no idea he had hit Hollywood, although he was still in B movies. To prevent potentially awkward moments for our respective partners should he recognize me and we stop to talk, I looked down as he passed by, but couldn't resist looking back, and to my surprise, he too had turned. Our eyes locked, I smiled in recognition, he smiled back, and we continued on our ways. Do I regret our relationship not having grown to the next level? With Kermit, yes. With the tender young man I knew, definitely yes. With the tabloid-fodder megastar, no. With hair-flinging Cher, definitely not.

> 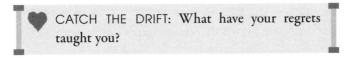 CATCH THE DRIFT: What have your regrets taught you?

Regrets Should Not Rule

> "I think everybody should get rich and famous and do everything they ever dreamed of so they can see that it's not the answer."
> —JIM CARREY[9]

It appears Jimmy did regret some choices after all. Regrets are not necessarily a bad thing! Regrets about choices we've made or not made can make us wiser if we mine the depths of experience to discover the wisdom there. For instance, regrets can alert us to desires and values and transmit information about the direction that we want to head in the future. Do you want to marry? If so, what type of person do you need to avoid or try to meet? Shy frogs? Outgoing porcines? If we listen to our regrets concerning past relationships, we may indeed learn more about who *is* right for us, or if we are even ready or right for others.

Confronting regret means to remember what you have faced before to see how an experience might inform you about your current dilemma or desires so that you can avoid repeating a mistake or poor choice. For example, if you were abused in your previous relationship, you might recall what about that person, in his character, might signal you today as traits to avoid in a suitor. Or, if you constantly pushed your spouse away or sabotaged your own happiness, you might search or revisit the past for events or symptoms that may have caused this repetitively destructive behavior. It's amazing how our history can impact or even dictate how we live and who we are today; things can become so ingrained in us that reactions become automatic.

Not always about negative things, regrets can also be about past glories, better days, happier times. In my first marriage with Phil, whom I was with for 12 years before Nathan, we had few financial worries, and we seldom fought. I have never laughed as much as I did in my time with Jimmy. It would have been easy to grow resentful in comparing what was then to my reality with Nathan—frequent fighting and struggle—and to my prospects for a happy future, and I admit, I did loiter a few times in those earlier glories when things grew particularly difficult.

This caused me to regret what I perceived as my present, my allotment, and my future. Regret of the future is disguised as worry or unfounded imaginations. Newly single, you might be drowning in: What if I'm single for the rest of my life? My sister, just last week, tearfully expressed this fear when we talked on the phone following her receiving a "Dear Jane" letter.

Such regrets can leave us rootless and feeling unsettled; they rule the moment, and if we are not careful may lead to negative reactions or poor choices that could multiply our regret lode, enslaving us to time, to circumstances, leading us to apathy, passivity, fear, depression, stagnation, or the wrong person; not good for you or your children and a surefire way to guarantee forever singleness or added heartbreak! We may imagine everything to go wrong and thus fear taking the steps we need to take to get what we want. In the meantime, opportunity passes by.

 CATCH THE DRIFT: If we desire marriage again, heck, even a great date, we need to do things to get there. We increase the potential of finding healthy love again by pressing on in the present free of unhealthy thinking and emotionally binding ties. When we deal with past regrets wisely, we are creating favorable current conditions that will help us avoid future regrets, and fill us with faith. What is binding you? Are you willing to move ahead?

B-r-e-a-t-h-e, You're Normal!

Take heart. Regrets *are* normal. If someone tells me that he or she lives without regret I'm apt to think that person has lived a perfect life having made no bad decisions (unlikely), or has never been victim of a bad decision made by another, or has no life. To regret something is to revisit past events or decisions, and compare them to what might have or should have or could have been and wishing they had been different. It is like taking a back road rife with obstacles that may cause delay. Life present has enough obstacles to deal with! Let me tell you, I have had a life filled with regrets that still at times can bring on sudden waterworks or trembling, but I had to learn to let them go to move on into healthier relationships all the way around—with coworkers, friends, and family members. Not that I denied or minimized the severity of some of the things that happened; but I came to terms with each regret and released the pain, thus ending the distortion that they created in my life. I also finally made peace with my own flawed self, my thoughts, my heart, and other people. I forgave myself and forgave those who had hurt me, whether intentionally or unintentionally. If a regret interferes with my happiness or future, if I am more consumed by the should haves and would haves than I am by my present, I take stock to determine how much my regret is costing me, my family, and my future.

Better to Light a Candle (Than Curse the Darkness)

Interestingly, in Kermit's "Bein' Green"[10] song, the lovable frog expresses his regret about his color, wishing himself another hue. But something incredible happens as a result of exposing his regret; it leads him to the truth about himself: Being green can be beautiful! "Green can be big, like a mountain, or important, like a river, or tall, like a tree."[11]

In the end, Kermie decides he is happy with his greenness and embraces it. "It's beautiful," he sings, "and I think it's what I want to be."[12]

Regret led Kermit to knowledge. Knowledge to understanding. Understanding to realization. And, realization to a stronger sense of identity, which is probably why Miss Piggy pursued him so! Ultimately, it changed the conditions in his life.

A regret about a past relationship, if harnessed right, has the same amazing potential as fear does to transform negative thought processes, lead you to the truth, and bring you into a place of confidence in who you are, and as a result, you will not have to chase happiness, it will pursue you. As you heal, and grow through regret, you will become that flashy sparkle in the water that catches the eye of someone special, that causes that person to reach down, gather you all up as a package, to forever cherish as treasure. You do this by working through your regrets now, sooner than later. Ribbeting chapter, isn't it?

Take Stock

Have you evaluated your regrets? If so, what effect have they had on you? Your situation? Your outlook? How much joy have your regrets pilfered? Who do you need to forgive? Have you forgiven yourself? Moreover:

- What are your regrets costing you?
- Which ones still linger?
- Of those regrets, which were in your control, and which were not?
- Are you willing to let them go?
- Are the children OK?

CATCH THE DRIFT: If you find yourself asking many questions of yourself about why bad things have happened in your relationships, congratulations. You are alive, and within you remains at least a seed of desire to see your dreams bloom to fulfillment. A question is like a pinch that awakens us to thoughts about the unknown, that focuses our attention, and that gives us a cliff edge to hang onto as we heal as well as a hope-on-a-rope with which to pull ourselves into a better future. Moreover, the more profound our questions—the more awesome the journey, the more amazing the renewal, the greater the revelations and understandings, and hence, the greater the possibilities. So go ahead, keep the questions flowing to yourself about yourself because discovering the root of you will in time clear a path to help you find the most perfect love and co-parenting partner for you.

Below the Surface

Date: _____

Are my children OK?
_____
_____
_____
_____

What are their fears?
_____
_____
_____
_____

What do they need?
_____
_____
_____
_____

Who or what is my ultimate concern right now?
_____
_____
_____
_____

What has happened to me?
_____
_____
_____
_____

What is happening to me?
_____
_____
_____
_____

What's next?
_____
_____
_____
_____

What do I really want?
_____
_____
_____
_____

Why am I worried?
_____
_____
_____
_____

What am I most afraid of?
_____
_____
_____
_____

What is deep down inside of me that I haven't brought forth yet?
_____
_____

___

What do I have to offer?

___

___

What truths or lies have shaped my perceptions of me?

___

___

How faithful am I to my yearnings?

___

___

What sacrifices have I made?

___

___

Who has sacrificed for me?

___

___

What am I grateful for?

___

Who can I reach out to?

Who is the top person in my support network?

Who do I need to forgive?

Endnotes

1. From a quote by Terri Guillemets, "Life's not always fair. Sometimes you can get a splinter even sliding down a rainbow."

2. Originally titled "Green," "Bein' Green" was written by Joe Raposo (Jonico Music Inc. and Green Fox Music, Inc., 1970) for the first season of *Sesame Street*; www.seasamestreet.org.

3. Part of a quote by Louis Adamic: "My grandfather always said that living is like licking honey off a thorn." Quoted at

http://thinkexist.com/quotation/my_grandfather_always_said_that_living_is_like/213444.html.

4. Name changed to protect his privacy. This is my son's father.
5. This is my first "public" reveal. It is not now, and never has been, my intention to exploit Jim Carrey in any way. Moreover, I do not seek to gossip, nor do I seek attention, notoriety, or gain of any kind. Our relationship, as brief as it was, and as young as we were, greatly impacted my life before Jim's rise to fame, taught me much, and its story and pertinent parts merits inclusion.
6. My memory is a little unclear whether the check was for $1 million or $10 million, but I do believe it was for the latter.
7. See stanza lyrics at start of chapter.
8. My first husband—we were married for 11 years. We had no children together.
9. Jim Carrey, *Reader's Digest* (March 2006), 81, in "Quotable Quotes." It is also available at: http://www.rd.com/clean-jokes-and-laughs/7000125/article7000125.html.
10. Raposo, "Bein' Green."
11. *Ibid.*
12. *Ibid.*

Chapter Three

Wake Up and Smell the Double Mocha Latte!

Creating More Favorable Heart Conditions

> *Sometimes I lie awake at night, and I ask, 'Where have I gone wrong?' Then a voice says to me, 'This is going to take more than one night.'*
>
> —CHARLIE BROWN[1]

At 20 and a not-yet-married single, I was hired by a Canadian airline as a flight attendant and was sent out west to Vancouver for two months of training. Upon graduation from in-flight school, I would be permanently relocated to either Montreal (my hometown and first choice), Toronto, or remain in Vancouver (my last choice). Having lived all my life in Montreal, I was dismayed to learn that I would be based in Vancouver, 2,000 miles away from home! Young, naive, a little scared, and vulnerable, I met "Tom the Opportunist," who offered to rent me a room in a house he shared with two people. Days after I moved in, he pursued more than friendship, and, because I was uncomfortable with being alone and on my own in a strange city, I acquiesced, and before I knew it, we were a couple. About a week into our relationship, I discovered he was an alcoholic. About two weeks into it, a mean alcoholic. He dangled manipulative threats: "If you leave, where will you go? You can't possibly survive on your own." A month and a black eye later, I ran! Scooted butt. Believe me, there are a whole lot of costly regrets packed in that story. What was I thinking?

> He dangled manipulative threats: "If you leave, where will you go? You can't possibly survive on your own."

Before I could even slap the steak on the eye, I met Phil. Twelve years older than me, he was a gentle, kind, and sympathetic type, the opposite of Tom. Phil was divorced after marrying young; his children lived with their mother. I remember thinking of him as my knight riding in on a white and spectacular horse. A savior of sorts. Someone who would save me from myself, bad men, and any further poor choices on my part! Within six months, we were married. Things were good for many years. We lived the "good" life and for the most part had few squabbles. But unfortunate circumstances caused the relationship to turn.

We stopped communicating, playing, loving. Phil and I went to couples' and one-on-one counseling, tried our best to save the marriage, but our hurts were blinders that prevented us from seeing our problems and me from believing that we could survive even another year together. After 11 years of marriage, one day, while he was out of town, I packed my bags and left.

Perhaps at the time, deep down inside, I knew it was not the right choice, but a part of me had hoped that my leaving would create change, so I did what I thought was best, in my heart believing it would be temporary. I loved him dearly. For a time, I drowned in hurtful regret, wrestled with unlovability issues, and "if only I had" guilty feelings. Remaining in the doldrums made me vulnerable to a rebound relationship, which would find its foundation built on regret-caused fear. Had I known then what I know now about men and their challenges in sharing their feelings, and had I communicated my feelings to Phil in a way that he would understand, I am certain we would be together today.

Mutual regret eventually and many years later brought Phil and I together as best friends, and by that time, thankfully so, we both had grown. We've had long, retrospective and heartfelt talks concerning our regrets. Although we still wonder what would have happened had we tried harder, pushed harder, petitioned harder, worked harder at saving our marriage, we have forgiven each other, we have learned to accept our mistakes, we have celebrated the time we had together, and we have both moved on with greater wisdom, maturity, and resolve not to repeat those misjudgments or omissions in our respective romantic relationships. It's ironic (and sad) that we communicate better now than we did in marriage. I only wish that we had arrived at that juncture before I jumped into my next marriage.

Create Favorable Conditions Now

Although time naturally tempers some regrets, they tend to multiply, perpetuate, or compound if we do not deal with them. Many regrets manifest as worry, and this worry dragged me down before I even got up in the morning when my second marriage crashed head-on in the rocks. There was much more at stake this time around. A child.

Suddenly single, for weeks, lonely, scared, and full of regrets, I worried: Would DS ever have a right example of love and marriage to take with him into his own life? Would I ever be desired again? And oh, would I ever again experience intimate union in marriage, ooh la-la? I loved the lovemaking, that blending of pleasant feelings into a masterpiece of oneness in love. Sigh. Some days I'd just bury my head in my pillow and weep for what could have and should have been. But for DS's sake, I had to pull myself together, and quick.

What we do *now* creates the conditions for future events. As a parent, you already know this. If you want your children to grow up as secure adults, you love on them majorly now. In the same way, if they are to become independent of you and able to survive on their own, you have to send them to school now. If your child grows up feeling unlovable, what do you think of her marriage prospects as an adult? If your child is uneducated? Hence, if you desire a healthy relationship or successful remarriage, appropriate positive conditions have to be implemented. Drowning in the poor conditions of the present will not favorably impact a favorable outcome.

Recycle Opportunities

We cannot really change the past but we can change our attitude concerning it, we can change our understanding of it, and we can change what we do with it. We can change the effect of the past, and that, in my opinion, is as good as changing the event. The bend in the road is only the end of the road if we refuse to take the turn.[2] How we react emotionally, psychologically, even physically (get out of your pajamas already) determines how the event influences us today, *now*.

> The bend in the road is only the end of the road if we refuse to take the turn.

Someone once said, *"Regret is to the emotions as the open flame is to the hand. Feel the pain, learn the lesson, [heal], move on."*[3] I needed to ask, before pursing a relationship: "How can what happened and its hurts (the result of my poor choice, that of another, or of something out of my control) work *for* me rather than against me?" Coming to terms with it, looking at it squarely, creates an opportunity to grow and learn. Regret can also reveal what you most value, your deepest desires, what is most important to you and even *recycle* opportunities. If you take time evaluating your greatest "if onlys," likely, you will see a common thread in them that will reveal what is truly important to you. Once revealed, and when a choice aligned with your values presents or re-presents itself, you can confidently go for it because there is a lesser chance it will be a poor decision.

By the way, are the children OK?

Take Care of Lingering Regrets

An old Yiddish proverb says, *"A man is not old until his regrets take the place of his dreams."* Charles Dickens seemed to have concurred, saying, *"Regrets are the natural property of gray hairs."*[4] Likely those gray hairs belonged to Catherine, his wife, whom he dumped for his mistress.

Dickens fell in love with Catherine after his first romantic relationship ended badly. He married her, and they had ten children. Overwhelmed with her responsibilities as a mother to such a large brood and as wife to one of the most famous men on the planet, Catherine employed her sister Georgina to help out, and she eventually ran the Dickens's household. Charles grew resentful of his wife, seeing the children and the financial burden they caused, and his wife's "inability" to cope as mother and dutiful wife as *her* fault. He also began to indicate that she was far from his intellectual equal (grrr).

His discontent with her flaws led him back into the arms of his first love, but Ellen, also having married, did not live up to his romantic memories and nothing came of their reunion. He met another woman, and she became his mistress until his death. Life with his wife seemed even more miserable after meeting her, and they took separate bedrooms. One day, he arranged to have a bracelet that he had bought delivered to Ellen, but it was accidentally delivered to Catherine, who of course then knew of his affair. Although he denied it, they were legally separated. In a letter to a friend as they separated, Dickens wrote, "Poor Catherine and I are not made for each other, and there is no help for it. It is not only that she makes me uneasy and unhappy, but that I make her so, too—and much more so." Even considering his confession, he took the children and did not encourage their visiting her. Catherine lived another 20 years alone, deprived of the role of mother and wife, and it is said that she never seemed to recover from the marriage breakup.[5]

I wonder, had she been able to surmount the regrets of her failed marriage, would Catherine have had the resolve to fight for custody of her children? Would she have met someone and remarried?

Only when I dealt with the negative byproducts of unresolved regret could I step toward freedom; only then would the doors open to a newer, lighter, easy and breezy and more beautiful life! For both DS and I! Conversely, unresolved or ongoing guilt, unforgiveness, self-pity, sadness, pain, vindictiveness, self-righteousness, and the incessant "What was I thinking?" almost crushed our dreams.

I really had no choice but to let go; it wasn't only my life at stake, I had my child to think about, and his dreams and hopes for a good future. Whenever I hesitated, it was only because of a lack of understanding or not knowing how to let something go.

 CATCH THE DRIFT: Do you have a burdensome regret? Perhaps you've lost a spouse to death and you are regretting things you should have said or done. Perhaps this regret has prevented you from being able to grieve. Maybe in your loss, you went wild for a time, or perhaps you haven't been there for your children. Are there things you've done but wish you hadn't? Things you did not do but wish you had? Are you wishing you had heeded your mother's warning about Harry? Is there something another has done that you wish she hadn't, or something you wished she had done? Have you been weighed down by tragedy, such as an untimely death or illness of a loved one, an accident? Even your circumstances—the loss of love, family, your home—can cause regret. Likewise, comparing your life to the life of another whom you view as more successful, beautiful, and blessed than you are can cause more regret, which will negatively affect your self-esteem and confidence. "High self-esteem isn't a luxury," says Jack Canfield, of *Chicken Soup for the Soul* fame. "It's a necessity for anyone who has important goals to achieve."[6]

Choose to Let Go

Choosing to let go is something only you can do, for your regrets belong to you, and nobody else. It may seem at times as if they belong to all involved, but they are yours, just as possibility belongs to you!

How often do you say or think:

- If I could just...do it over...
- If only he hadn't (done this, said that)...
- Oh why oh why didn't (I/he/she)...
- I should have...could have...and then I would have or be..."
- I'd give anything if only...
- I wish things were different...

Large or small we always have the same options: hang on to regrets or release them. In the words of Dr. Seuss: "You have brains in your head. You have feet in your shoes. You can steer yourself in any direction you choose. You're on your own. And you know what you know. You are the [one] who'll decide where to go."[7]

Take heart! You already have practice in letting go of regret, small regrets happen every day, and the older you are, the more you have had. How often I've regretted eating that third quarter-pounder-with-cheese in a week, trying out a chi-chi new hair style, or embarking on a household project that I knew required a professional, just for not-so-serious starters. These smaller "oops" regrets are easier to manage and easier to move on from, granted, with lesser consequences, repercussions, or negative outflows. We do not tend to dote on those regrets; often, I even find myself laughing at them. Regrets, no matter how trivial or burdensome, can either keep reminding us of our mistakes or keep reminding us of the lessons we have learned through them, so that we don't repeat the mistake.

> CATCH THE DRIFT: Start small, with the petty stuff, the non life-altering or life-threatening regrets. When you can make peace with the lesser events or circumstances out of your control, you will be able to deal with the larger regrets. Letting go immediately feels good, and just may spur you on to purge the heavier regrets. This will do more wonders for your smile than the best tooth whitener. Our children need parents who smile and celebrate life, even if toothless.

Identify Symptoms of Prolonged or Burdensome Regret

Don't let regret rule your life because you'll regret it one day if you do. Practice awareness of the symptoms of regret so that you can catch it as it arises before it destroys your emotional, spiritual, and even physical well-being and chances for love. Although it is natural to experience these feelings and reactions, prolonged, they may signal a problem. Potential symptoms: self-pity, jealousy, anger, worry, resentfulness, insecurity, depression, lethargy, fear, high blood pressure, hostility.

Evaluate Whether You Are Over Your Past Relationship

Letting go so that you can move on can be one of the greatest challenges. Dealing with regret, the passing of time, and forgiveness can help you heal and open your heart to new love. But how do you really know you have truly released him or her? For me with Nathan, whom I see often because we share custody of our son, I discovered the release when I forgave him. It did not happen overnight; it took seventy-times-seven or more times to remove the many links in the chain of unforgiveness that kept me bound in feelings of ill will. Miraculously, fonder memories of our earlier years surfaced, such as the joy we shared when DS was born, rather than the more hurtful times. Until the overwhelming hurt and sadness left, until I could stop thinking of him as a beast, a schmuck, I was still attached to him, albeit in an unhealthy way. I can truly say today that I love him as a human being, and for the gift he gave me of our son.

When Nathan and I first got together, for months I could not get Phil out of my mind, the regret, intense. I constantly wondered where he was, what he was doing, and my thoughts blurred my concentration on our relationship, and perspective. Although it is normal to think of a newly departed spouse often at first, if the smallest things still continually remind you of him, conversely, if you're stalking him, if you're obsessed in any way, especially with getting back together, or, in the case of a loss through death, you feel you simply cannot go on without him, likely you are not ready for new love; and in both instances, especially if you have frequent thoughts of death, you need counseling.

Accept Responsibility Where Applicable

In several of my failed relationships, it would have been much easier to lay blame on the other; but in reality, I made choices that were not that great. Accepting responsibility strengthened and motivated me to better evaluate the decisions I make today. I can admit and confess now when things are my fault, as being my fault, without laying blame on God, circumstances, others, bad luck, or hormones!

Forgive

Forgiveness played a large part in my healing, in my release of sorrows, in my release from Nathan, and in my freedom to love again. Someone once wisely said, "A woman who can't forgive should never have more than a nodding acquaintance with a man."[8] Until I could forgive him, I really didn't even have the moral right to move on because, in effect, I was still bound to him. Forgiving Nathan especially was difficult but I had to cough up the unforgiveness fur ball or remain shackled to a litter box of misery. So too, if someone is still hurting you, there is power in forgiving as you are being crucified. This does not mean that you are condoning someone's actions or that you should not take steps necessary to stop the abuse, but the sooner we can forgive, the less likely it is that we will do or say something that we will at some point regret.

Forgiveness is vital no matter the injustice or cruelty dealt us. Forgiveness is a spirit of love that goes beyond justice. Justice may preserve our dignity but it does not sustain it. Love, however, does. Forgiving Nathan was the most significant factor in my healing, in my son's healing, and in our moving on. Without forgiveness, all I could think of was revenge, hateful thoughts, vengeful emotions. I could not change the past but I could change the present. The best way to do that was to decide to forgive and experience the release of dangerous cargo.

> Justice may preserve our dignity but it does not sustain it.

CATCH THE DRIFT: Forgiving someone does not mean you've given in, and certainly does not mean you condone or approve a wrongdoing. Nor does it give someone a green light to keep hurting you. It is not approval of a misdoing, and it does not mean you are subjecting yourself to more harm. You can forgive and still be clear about your boundaries. Henry Ward Beecher said, "Forgiveness oughtt to be like a canceled note, torn in two, and burned up."[9]

Forgiveness released me from harmful emotions. It freed me to love again because prior I was emotionally and mentally invested in what had happened. We tie ourselves to situations and people when we hate or resent them. Bitterness binds us to them, strengthens our connection, and causes grey hair and wrinkles! It is said that to forgive is to set a prisoner free and discover that the prisoner was you. On the other hand, forgiveness can lead to empathy and even compassion toward the offender. Forgiving can be extremely difficult, but it is essential to being able to move beyond the past. When we don't forgive those who hurt us so badly, we only succeed in dragging them with us into our future.

How do you know if you need to forgive someone? Some clues are: You react in anger to the smallest slights, or you are consumed by thoughts of justice, revenge, or punishment, or you are coping with a hurt with alcohol, drugs, or excessive busyness, or you are the guest of honor at your own pity party.

Seek Understanding, Meaning, and Value

I sought meaning and value in regrets because, as I earlier noted, every regret, past, present, or future, has a lesson. You just have to find it. When you do the same, you will gain greater wisdom and understanding for the next regret. With the devastation surrounding my breakup with Nathan, my mistrust issue (disguised as low self-esteem) gained some exposure, but I didn't deal with it until it broke loose with fury after the breakup of yet another rebound relationship, while I was still vulnerable, and it almost crushed me for good. I determined that I would never trust anyone ever again.

This challenge had likely stalked me my whole life, gathering steam as this young foster child moved from home to home, and as I moved from failed relationship to failed relationship—with Phil and Nathan, and with the most recent disaster as well. It had developed into a negative thought process, the result of something I learned in childhood and in previous relationships that I had to *learn to unlearn*, if that makes sense.

For the most part, I've let go of those regrets, and with them, the hurt and mistrust. Which brings me to the second part of this step: knowing why I was letting go, and stating or journaling the reason to myself. I let go because I wanted to be free to trust again, to love again. I desired to be free of those regrets because prolonged bitterness or pain or mistrust eventually would badly impact my son as it sickened me. It was vital, therefore, that I loosen regret's claws on my life.

Are you ready to let go, to forgive? What's your motivation?

Make Amends

I had to learn and take the necessary steps to mend things—for instance, unkind things I've said in my hurt and pain—and I've since mended many other similar fences that I have broken. I also sought to mend my ways concerning me! How often I told myself how worthless and unlovable I was. But hear and heed the words of Theodore Isaac Rubin:

> I must learn to love the fool in me, the one who feels too much, talks too much, takes too many chances, wins sometimes and loses often, lacks self-control, loves and hates, hurts and gets hurt, promises and breaks promises, laughs and cries.[10]

Regrets and the pains of our past teach us what we don't want, what we don't want to be, and where we don't want to go. We have to give ourselves time to discover the truths within them because this knowledge will not only make us wiser but also empower and equip us to break old unhealthy patterns and learn new healthier ones. Don't linger too long though, because regrets can haunt you, get you into the victim headspace, make you the star of your personal little soap opera. If this happens, you may need the help of a therapist, counselor, rabbi or pastor.

So listen, you are reading *The Single Parent's Guide to Love, Dating, and Relationships* because you are searching. Why not commit to living in the now with all its bumps, pains, dead ends, and possibilities! Father Alfred D'Souza in viewing the obstacles that he perceived got in the way of his experiencing real life, and in wondering when life for him would begin, discovered, "At last it dawned on me that these obstacles were my life."[11] Profound, eh?

Possibility in the past is regret, possibility in the future is destiny. Possibility greets you with the healing of regrets. When you purpose to stop camping on them, move off your island, and set about living for possibility, as your love affair with life is rekindled, you will be ready to fall in love again. In choosing to heal and learn from regrets, even sorrow, you are leaving defeat behind and entering into the lush and vibrant flow of real relationship possibility not only with others, but also with yourself.

Below the Surface

Date: _____

Are my children OK?

_____
_____
_____
_____

What are their fears?

_____
_____
_____
_____

What do they need?

_____
_____
_____
_____

Who or what is my ultimate concern right now?

_____
_____
_____

What has happened to me?

What is happening to me?

What's next?

What do I really want?

Why am I worried?

What am I most afraid of?

What is deep down inside of me that I haven't brought forth yet?

What do I have to offer?

What truths or lies have shaped my perceptions of me?

How faithful am I to my yearnings?

What sacrifices have I made?

Who has sacrificed for me?
_____
_____
_____
_____

What am I grateful for?
_____
_____
_____
_____

Who can I reach out to?
_____
_____
_____
_____

Who is the top person in my support network?
_____
_____
_____
_____

Who do I need to forgive?
_____
_____
_____
_____

Endnotes

1. Charles M. Schultz, Charlie Brown in "Peanuts," http://www.quotationspage.com/quote/29637.html.

2. From the saying (author unknown), "The bend of the road is not the end of the road unless you refuse to take the turn."
3. "Heal" is my addition to this anonymous quote.
4. Charles Dickens, quote found at http://www.famous-quotes.com/author.php?page=2&total=73&aid=2017.
5. Charles Dickens, The Gad's Hill Place: "The Marriage of Charles Dickens," www.perryweb.com/Dickens/life_marry.shtml.
6. Jack Canfield, *How to Build Self-Esteem: A Practical Process for Your Personal Growth* (Audiocassettes; Nightingale Conant Corp, 1989).
7. Dr. Seuss, *Oh, the Places You'll Go!* (New York: Random House, reprint ed. 1990).
8. Quote attributed to Ed Howe. See, for example, http://www.worldofquotes.com/topic/Forgiveness/2/index.html.
9. The full quote from Henry Ward Beecher is, "I can forgive, but I cannot forget, is only another way of saying, I will not forgive. Forgiveness ought to be like a canceled note—torn in two, and burned up, so that it never can be shown against one." See http://www.worldofquotes.com/topic/Forgiveness/2/index.html.
10. Theodore Isaac Rubin, quoted at http://www.goodreads.com/author/quotes/1407057.Theodore_Isaac_Rubin.
11. Father Alfred D'Souza, quoted at http://thinkexist.com/quotation/for-a-long-time-it-had-seemed-to-me-that-life-was/411049.html.

Chapter Four

One Doesn't Have to Be the Loneliest Number

How to Be Singularly Spectacular

"Look, I don't want to wax philosophic, but I will say that if you're alive you've got to flap your arms and legs, you've got to jump around a lot, for life is the very opposite of death, and therefore you must at least think noisy and colorfully, or you're not alive."
—Mel Brooks[1]

Unless we can learn how to be happily and joyfully single, there is little chance we will find the love we crave. Do you really know who you are? Did you lose yourself somewhere? Years ago I met a woman, 55 years old, whose husband of 36 years left her for a younger woman.

The person she thought she would share her entire life with was suddenly out of the picture, and her world as she knew it was over. She had so merged her identity with his—for so long she felt half of a couple—that she could not imagine continuing as a whole individual. She did not know if she had strength enough to care for herself without his help. In a society defined by relationships, she was ashamed of her singlehood, and terrified just as I was as a newly single.

Time—more than she knew and in ways she could not foresee while in the early stages of recovery—would provide the emotional cushion that would allow her to put in the work to fight off her codependence and bring her back into that place of wholeness and confidence in who she was and what she was capable of. It would bring her to a place of becoming lovable by loving herself. However, it took time and effort on her part, as it did for me with my breakup, to heal and to feel good flying solo. Likewise, reinventing, cultivating, and enjoying ourselves as a single people was a necessary challenge that would ensure that we did not repeat mistakes or rush into other unhealthy relationships.

What Have You Done With You?

It took months after my sudden breakup with DS's father to grieve my losses, to heal, and to believe I was capable, lovable, or even worthy enough to find love again. In retrospect, I had allowed my relationship to define who I was; thus, I viewed the end of our marriage as the end of me. Feeling incomplete, and fearful of remaining incomplete, I was in danger of repeating this mistake, of finding someone who would define me, fill that piece of me that had broken off. While marriage is two people coming together to form a whole, it is not two halves joining, but two whole people with different strengths, gifts, and talents joining to complement each other, uniting to become a bigger whole—an incredible force in the world.

Until I could stop thinking of myself as a half and begin believing in myself and in growing as a complete and capable person in my own right, fear of my lack in any area: emotional, physical, spiritual, or financial would motivate my desperation to be married again. I would be seeking to use another person to fulfill my needs or to find someone who has what I either don't have or don't think I have, and once he gives it to me, what then? Would I be happy? Would the relationship hold?

In being needy and expecting fulfillment in a human being, we are setting ourselves up to find fault with a person who can never deliver what we hope he or she will. Thus, we are setting him or her up to make mistakes, and potentially sabotaging a relationship before it ever begins. You may think you've met your superman or superwoman, your Ken or Barbie, but at some point you'll have to give him or her permission to be human, and what you see might cause great letdown, which might cause the sizzle to fizzle, if you know what I mean! You'll never find the joy and peace you long for until you stop searching the planet for a Romeo or Juliet or human god or goddess who can fulfill your deepest longings or fix what is wrong in your life. Such a search is a wasteful use of your time, time better spent getting into the place where you are asking not "What can a person give me," but, "What can I give to him or her?" As Mother Teresa said, *"The success of love is in the loving—it is not in the result of loving."*² Something miraculous happens in that headspace—many of our perceived needs and pains vanish, and we feel more empowered to deal with the remaining ones.

> **In being needy and expecting fulfillment in a human being, we are setting ourselves up to find fault with a person who can never deliver what we hope he or she will.**

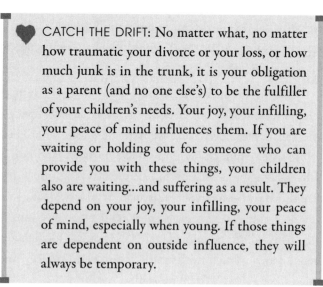

CATCH THE DRIFT: No matter what, no matter how traumatic your divorce or your loss, or how much junk is in the trunk, it is your obligation as a parent (and no one else's) to be the fulfiller of your children's needs. Your joy, your infilling, your peace of mind influences them. If you are waiting or holding out for someone who can provide you with these things, your children also are waiting...and suffering as a result. They depend on your joy, your infilling, your peace of mind, especially when young. If those things are dependent on outside influence, they will always be temporary.

Understandably, many single parents seek to fill the void of loneliness, but is our perceived need of companionship a result of not being in companionship with ourselves? Perhaps not even loving ourselves? Alternatively, perhaps we feel as if the loneliness would disappear if we were in relationship. It might for a time, but eventually loneliness will resurface, with a vengeance! The kind of loneliness that comes from a loveless marriage is one of the worst forms. The aches are felt so much more profoundly, the wounds, that much deeper when we seek to have our emotional needs met in marriage and they are not. Loneliness may have crept into your life long before you met your spouse, long before you lost your spouse, and if it was not dealt with then, for sure it is compounded in your loss.

I committed to a relationship with Nathan because at the time I felt unloved, and he wooed me so well. For a time, the relationship took that pain away, but because I hadn't yet dealt with the root of the self-esteem problem, I emotionally buckled the first time he verbally cut me down. That put much pressure not only on him, but also on the relationship.

 CATCH THE DRIFT: If we are convinced we are not good enough, we will have a difficult time accepting someone into our life who thinks we are the cat's meow. Until we get to that place of believing ourselves a catch, we will never believe it when someone tells us that we are.

It would have been far better to have dealt with my rejection issues before diving into a new relationship. When we are in pain, lonely, unhappy, or feeling needy, we may also forget the challenges involved in a relationship. We idealize it, see it as greener grass trumping our problems, as an answer to all of our woes. Again, this sets us up for disappointment because in all likelihood, unless the person is a corpse, he or she will also be undergoing a process of growth, as you are. You may meet the person at his or her peak, but there's always a valley between every mountain, as most single parents especially know. Moreover, that person might be in a valley when you meet, and you might dismiss him or her based on what you perceive you need, and miss out on a really great prospect who is simply in a natural process of growth, as we all are.

 CATCH THE DRIFT: Treat yourself as you have been treating your child in his loss. You have looked out for his best interest, treated him gently, tended his heart, given him time, actively been on his side, fed him well, given him chocolate. You need to be on your own side, too. Rest, treat yourself well, dive into the box!

In preparing yourself, in taking the time to mend, in taking the time to know yourself better, you are actually breaking down the walls of desperation and dissolving any calcifications of the heart that perhaps have held true love back; you from seeing it, knowing it, and experiencing it, and love from seeing, knowing, and experiencing you. Understandably, we erect these defenses to protect our bruises, our woundings, the darkness and ills of the heart. You are also giving an incredible gift to your children because you cannot give them what you yourself do not have. If you do not have peace, how can you exude it? If you do not have joy, how can you share it? If you do not know who you are, how can they know you?

The most important good changes in my healing time occurred in my attitude, in my emotions, and in my mindset. Surprise! As a result, I discovered that the single life following my divorce was full of advantage and possibility because I indeed became more attractive to people, with a brighter countenance that filled out most of my worry lines.

Not that marriage isn't ideal, or that the single life is substantially better, rather, that I suddenly understood that all people, no matter how close we are to them, no matter how much they love us, will disappoint us, and we, them. It is human nature. Therefore, I became aware of areas where I depended on Nathan for my happiness, for instance, when I should not have, where I lived vicariously through him rather than as a whole person beside a whole person. Single, I could test who I really was without influence to the contrary. And, I had to be true to myself. I had to learn to stand on my own in those newfound convictions so that in future relationship, the fear of loss would not assail me.

This meant that I needed to understand my personality better, explore my needs, and discover my true likes, dislikes, goals, dreams, and beliefs. In short, with the goal of personal growth. Single time matured me, gave me time to identify my desires, confront personal demons, explore inner strengths, grow spiritually, and learn self-sufficiency and personal responsibility. It ensured that my desire for change had not clouded any possibilities that our relationship could be saved.

Indeed, it even made me a more confident parent, and this favorably impacted DS. Some beauty treatment, and let me tell you, a gift to your future love! In a way, I was given another opportunity to do what I should have done before I tied the knot the first time.

> CATCH THE DRIFT: In which areas have you depended on another for your happiness? How can you learn to become more self-sufficient in this area? Pouring out your thoughts in a journal or in the dust on your coffeetable is helpful in the process of discovery and healing.

Before you rush in, heal, enjoy, and grow in your new singleness; discover you and fill up that half of yourself that you perceive is missing. Indulge in the things you enjoyed, did solo before but gave up in marriage, like eating a chocolate bar for breakfast when you were running late for work, or stopping at all garage sales on your way to visit Aunt Martha in Connecticut, or going to bed with curlers, or leaving the tube off the toothpaste, or leaving the toilet seat up or down, or eating cookies in bed, or watching Monday Night Football reruns. Don't be in such a rush for a ring. Enjoy this time while you have it. Revel in your time of aloneness, hang out in your sweatpants, watch what you want to watch on television, raise the children your way (I trust it is the right way), turn up the volume on *So You Think You Can Dance,* and dance! Spend the time you spent with your spouse with your children, doing things with them that you have never done before. Go back to school, or catch up with visits to your extended family members. Bonus: They will feed you! And the children! They may even send you home with food! They may even offer to babysit!

Take time first to get grounded; it won't help to avoid the pain by rushing into a new relationship; eventually the pain will catch up to you. Deconstruct your previous relationship, break it down into parts: your part and the other person's part. Where did you go wrong? Where did she or he go wrong? Did you sweat the small stuff? Was he too reactive? Did you expect too much? Take responsibility for your end of things, and determine how not to go there again. Discover mistakes that you do not want to repeat, and make a pact with yourself to avoid them.

Use your single time to heal, to learn by your pain, to be free of it, to lose those extra pounds, and to understand yourself. Listen, if you love or care for someone, you try to find out all you can about him or her, right? Before you marry and move in and live forever together, you google him or her, right? You check out the Classmates.com page. You visit Facebook or MySpace. You call your ex-hood-turned-cop-third-cousin-twice-removed Vinny, and get the scoop. As a single living by yourself, you should be getting the scoop, good or bad, on *yourself.* Yes, on you! Ask yourself the same questions you would ask of a potential love interest.

Am I completely over him? Would I ever go back? What is our relationship like now, apart? Is it friendly? If not, why? What do I love? What do I enjoy? What are my dreams? What or who has influenced my life for good or bad, and why? What are my flaws? How do I want to be treated? Do I want more children? Do I want a relationship, or am I really searching for someone who will give me financial security? Am I overneedy? Ask yourself, Hey Good Looking, whatcha got cooking? What are my dreams for my future? What are the defining moments in my life that have made me who I am? What are my weaknesses, and is there a way I can turn them for me, not against me...into strengths?

Also ask yourself questions about your children. What is my son like? What are his needs? Is he ready for change yet? Is he OK? Assess your answers.

You may still be emotionally attached to your spouse. Clues may be that you hate him, fear him, still keep in close touch with your cousin Vinny, or, conversely, you cannot stand thinking of him with another person; he's always on your mind. Your child might need more "you" time, some counseling, or more time to adjust.

Open your heart and ask yourself, "Who do I want?" This is a prime time of discovery, especially if you have experienced many heartbreaking relationships, because you will ascertain it through contrast and your experiences.

If you are unable to answer certain questions, if you are still looking into the mirror and lamenting, "Who are you, and what have you done with me?" chances are, you are not ready for a new love relationship, you still need more *you* time.

Healing the Now

Reconstructing your sense of wholeness, getting past the pain, the martyrdom, the tears of deprecation, processing the loss, recreating a sense of family wholeness, helping your children heal, is a delicate and sometimes long process but never fruitless. Pain, fear, even the loss of a dream can grow us and strengthen and empower us for major, good transformation. When I felt whole, when I stopped defining myself through another, or by my worst moments, when I was able to look back and say, "This happened. It was hard. It was painful. It almost destroyed me. But it is not who I am; it is not how things will be. It is not my excuse. It is not my badge," this is when I began to thrive as a single parent, as a single woman. And yes, Daddy, you can thrive as a single man. Taking the time to heal, understanding that we don't heal the past but the now, using the past as a tool to shape rather than define, understanding that life is not a game show where one mistake wipes out all the right answers or good things that have happened. Understanding that life is not a test requiring an A, and anything less is a failure. This is what brought breakthrough and love to my life. You give it your best, and even if you only receive a 52 percent on the exam of life, even if you got 48 wrong, you got the rest right, and that is worth celebrating and moving forward with.

Checklist:

☐ Are the children OK?

- ☐ Have I identified what truly frightens me? Why I am afraid?

- ☐ Have I evaluated my self-talk? What is it saying?

- ☐ Have I identified lies, discovered the truth?

- ☐ Have I looked back on my life to evaluate the things I have successfully overcome to empower me for the challenges of today?

- ☐ Can I face those fears? Or, strategize to overcome them?

- ☐ Am I willing to release the past and concentrate on the future?

- ☐ Have I asked myself what I want?

- ☐ Am I expecting fulfillment through another person?

- ☐ Have I chosen to believe that my future might be better than my past?

- ☐ Have I chosen to be optimistic and hopeful?

- ☐ Have I accepted uncertainty as a fact of life?

- ☐ Have I checked my attitude?

- ☐ Am I truly over my last relationship?

- ☐ Have I strengthened my support system?

- ☐ Do I believe I can do it on my own, forever if necessary?

In Preparation...

Don't Retreat

Although it is necessary and healthy to seek time alone to grieve, heal, and come to terms with things, extended periods of isolation are not healthy. Interestingly, recent research has proposed that isolation is a consequence of being lonely.[3] The same research cites that loneliness is also contagious, those who are lonely tend to share their loneliness with others, and on the whole, tend toward more negative social interactions. Thus, your loneliness may affect your ability to find a new spouse.

If true, this would also mean that your children may catch your loneliness. If you are isolated, they are, too. If you cannot get along with others, nor will they. Surround yourself with loved ones who can give you support and uplift you. A good support system is vital and beneficial to you and your children. Don't forget, a counselor can help as well.

Reach out to family and friends. A surefire way to find love again is to show love to others, and regardless of your love life status, you will always need support. Look up old and safe friends who knew you before you married, and reconnect. They may just be able to help you rediscover your single self, having known you as a single. Additionally, this transition period provides a great opportunity to clear up those regrets, to refresh, to get healthy. All of these things you are doing will prepare you for your soulmate.

Get to Know Your Child

This is a vital time to mine the depths of your child's heart, to focus on bringing her back to that springtime place of childhood revelry, the joy of childhood, of innocence, which so often children lose as a result of a divorce or death of a parent. This is as bad if not worse than a monster in the closet, since it's real. Quality time now will increase her feelings of security, raise her self-esteem, and ease her anger, anguish, doubts, guilt, or loneliness. Engage, play, talk, listen, walk, focus. Create a secure environment for her. Does she need more? Does she need counseling? Is she OK? Is she secure in your love? In the other parent's love? Have you given her too much adult responsibility? What are her fears? Handle them now. Help her heal. Help her move on into a bright future with you. In passionately pursuing relationship with your child now, in building a sense of togetherness, future transitions will be much easier for her to handle and accept. (Please check out *The Single Parent's Guide to Raising Godly Children,* where I devote chapters to helping you help your children heal and feel good about themselves.[4])

Pursue a Passion

Yes, it will be difficult to find time in your busy schedule to pursue a dream, to practice a passion, but you just may discover, as you concentrate on you again, new purpose, new resolve. You are less likely to feel as lonely. Involving yourself in a hobby or activity is a perfect opportunity to rediscover who you are and what you enjoy in life. Be careful not to use your passion as a means of escape to avoid pain or loneliness; you do have to give yourself the chance to adjust to the reality of singleness and to learning how to live with yourself in comfort. Caveat: Never let it trump your personal quality time with your children.

Below the Surface

Date: _____

Are my children OK?

_____
_____
_____

What are their fears?

_____
_____
_____

What do they need?

_____

_____
_____
_____

Who or what is my ultimate concern right now?
_____
_____
_____

What has happened to me?
_____
_____
_____

What is happening to me?
_____
_____
_____

What's next?
_____
_____
_____

What do I really want?
_____
_____
_____

Why am I worried?

What am I most afraid of?

What is deep down inside of me that I haven't brought forth yet?

What do I have to offer?

What truths or lies have shaped my perceptions of me?

How faithful am I to my yearnings?

What sacrifices have I made?

Who has sacrificed for me?

What am I grateful for?

Who can I reach out to?

Who is the top person in my support network?

Who do I need to forgive?

Endnotes

1. Mel Brooks, quoted at http://thinkexist.com/quotes/Mel_Brooks/.
2. Mother Teresa of Calcutta, quoted at http://thinkexist.com/quotes/mother_teresa_of_calcutta/3.html.
3. ABC News/Health, http://abcnews.go.com/Health/DepressionNews/loneliness-contagious-researchers/story?id=9211377; Video and accompanying article: "Is Loneliness Contagious?" by Dan Childs and Lauren Cox, ABC News Medical Unit, December 1, 2009. Accessed May 28, 2010.
4. *The Single Parent's Guide to Raising Godly Children* (Shippensburg, PA: Destiny Image, 2010).

PART TWO

Finding The Perfect Person For The Real You

Chapter Five

I Beg Your Pardon, I Never Promised You a Rose Garden

Avoiding Regrets in Your Search for Love

> "Perfect love is rare indeed—for to be a lover will require that you continually have the subtlety of the very wise, the flexibility of the child, the sensitivity of the artist, the understanding of the philosopher, the acceptance of the saint, the tolerance of the scholar and the fortitude of the certain."
> —Leo Buscaglia[1]

Are you searching for the perfect person or for the perfect person for you? Even if you find your dreamboat, he or she will never measure up to what you have imagined or hoped that person to be. There will always in some way or at some point, or in a certain fashion be regret, disappointment, or wondering, "What if I had chosen someone else?" Moreover, Richard Bandler said:

> When people don't know how to change something, they often start searching for a way to justify failure, rather than thinking about how they could try doing something different to make it work.[2]

Those "in the know" frequently ask me, "What if you and Jimmy had...don't you regret...." I cannot know what life as Mrs. Cable Guy would have dolled out. Just as I cannot know if my life with Nathan might have improved. I cannot know if, had I remained in the first marriage, that Phil and I would still be together today. I can imagine, but I can never know for sure. What would have happened had I not met the father of my son? This I don't even want to imagine because I am grateful for the result of choosing him and our ten years together in that he gave me a beautiful gift, my bright, wise, handsome DS whom I adore, cherish, and love so immeasurably, I cannot even think of life without him. The pain was worth it in the long run.

Most Decisions Have a "What If" Aftermath

This is true of every choice we make or path we take, and we have to accept it: things don't usually happen in the way we've conjured its outcome. To illustrate simply, I recall my experience shopping for a car. My budget was $10,000 all in; including taxes. This meant I had about $8,000 toward the actual vehicle. I did my homework before I hit the dealerships just so that I would not be sold a lemon, took days beforehand pondering different models' benefits and risks. A single blonde woman with child in tow and walking into a dealership attracts car salespeople like a fly attracts a flyswatter. To their no-doubt surprise, I walked in knowing what I wanted, and after I heard their pitches and reasons why I should drop my hard-earned money on the hunk of rusted metal in the back lot, I narrowed my choices to two cars, PT Cruisers. And, do you think I could decide between them? The sensible 2005 midnight blue car had no extras, but it still had a year's warranty left, and only 18,000 miles, and after dishing out thousands of dollars in that past year in trying to fix Junk-a-poo, my old yuck Neon, this was attractive. The vanilla PT was gorgeous, though, a year older, 15,000 more miles on it, and all the bells and whistles. But no warranty left, and, it had a souped-up chrome muffler, which to me meant it had burned rubber. I wanted reliable wheels, and if possible, with bling.

Sensibility won over glitz; I chose the steak over the sizzle—but do you know what? The brakes failed me within a week, and I discovered a family of mice living under the hood, which explained why Gracie, my Jack Russell, kept going berserk in the car. To this day (I'm still driving Miss Daisy), I still wonder about that vanilla dream.

But our questions and decisions are infinitely tougher than that, aren't they? As single parents, we especially, whether single because of the death of a spouse, divorce, or separation, have more difficult decisions to make than easy ones because our children and their well-being factor largely. A single father may have to decide whether to propose marriage, a single mother to accept a proposal. Much is at stake! That candidate may become a surrogate parent to our children. Is he or she good enough? We have big decisions to make—like deciding to date again, like the right time to introduce a love to our children, like the decision to take that fish-sorting job in Alaska that would pay double and provide our kids with a college education, or like what I had to do: sell my precious dearly departed grandmother's valuable vase, which I had loved as a child and inherited, to pay the credit card bill. Those decisions at least give us choices. Perhaps there are several right times to introduce the children. There are other jobs, other things we can pawn, other ways to pay off the credit card. Other decisions may provide less options, like whether to buy food over paying the light bill. Again though, no matter the options, we usually base our decisions on our expectations, on our projected outcomes. If what we hope will happen does not happen, we regret the decision and wish we had taken a different tack.

> As single parents, we especially, whether single because of the death of a spouse, divorce, or separation, have more difficult decisions to make than easy ones.

Something not working out tends to make the right choice obvious, which is good, but this is when we tend to beat ourselves up the most: "How could we have been so... naive/ignorant/careless?" Veteran actor and the very debonair and romantic Maurice Chevalier discovered, likely through experience, *"Many a man has fallen in love with a girl in a light so dim he would not have chosen a suit by it."*[3]

> **Something not working out tends to make the right choice obvious.**

The more we revisit our regret, the more upset we are, increasingly, things will seem to spin out of control, and our emotional well-being will plunge, and suddenly, we'll find ourselves in analysis paralysis swimming in circles like a one-legged frog in a pond of hungry alligators. This is a recipe for self-pity, blaming others, and complaint, and if we are not careful, depression will swallow us whole. Forget dating! Nobody wants to date someone with an "oh poor little one-legged old me" mindset. Such a person can never be happy, or make someone happy. Show me a person with a victim mindset, and I'll show you a grumbler. If someone does date or marry such a person, he or she better have the name of a good psychiatrist or marriage counselor handy.

Use Caution With Insignificant or Hasty Decisions

We also have to be aware of what seems an insignificant, inconsequential, or hasty decision or choice because sometimes the smallest things can effect the greatest consequence or significance, for good or for bad.

Three months into my singleness I received an e-mail promoting an online Christian single's dating Web site. It provided a bold and convenient link and promised the earth. Against my better judgment, and spurred by loneliness, I clicked on it, and arrived at the site as a guest. While surfing through the many profiles, I stopped at a drop-dead gorgeous hunk, "Navy Man," from the eastern United States, who was searching only for "friendship." His wife had left him a year previously, and he was holding out for her return, but in the meantime, he was reaching out in his loneliness. I don't know what came over me—normally I'm a private, guarded person, but I contacted him. "Hi," I wrote, introducing myself. "I'm looking for friendship as well," not believing myself for a nano second!

At first we corresponded by e-mail because I had no plans to buy into a membership. Our relationship graduated to telephone calls, and eventually, a visit "in the name of friendship." Of course, romance blossomed. I was on the rebound, and Navy Man was, too, and did I mention, he was built—a cut above average! He also had an amazing sense of humor, and a gentle spirit for one so brawny. Most importantly, I felt he would protect me, and love me and DS forever. At least, he promised he would. When we decided to cross over from friendship, at first I was reluctant, still wounded and afraid of further wounding either DS or myself, but Navy Man vowed he felt a release from his wife, and that he would never hurt me or us. He guaranteed, promised me, that it was over and done with; that I could be confident in him, take the chance, that he was ready, that he had, in me, met the love of his life. He said he would love and cherish both me and my son. Blindsided by romance, we had not worked out the quirks, such as the fact that we lived in two separate countries, three thousand miles apart, that I shared custody of DS, that I could never leave DS for anyone or take him out of the country, that he would have to decide to move here, and the legalities and encumbrances and costs that distance and relocation entailed. Again, I was vulnerable, making decisions I thought were best, most in the best interest of DS, but I was still tender, so unhealed from the ungluing of my life.

Navy Man and I met in person for the first time in northern New York State. I arranged to stay with my foster parents, and would have him meet them as well. He arrived with a bouquet of exquisite roses, and, to my surprise, handed them to my foster mother! He passed muster, they loved him, and everything went smoothly, better than I could imagine. We had planned an October visit where Navy Man would get to know DS. For a time I forgot the ugly, the logistics; life was good—beautiful! Romance was alive! I set to work organizing my new suite, arranging *single occupancy* hotel accommodation for him, and preparing my son for meeting him. I could hardly wait! One night, however, one week to the day before he was to arrive, and three days before his divorce to Marie came through, Navy Man buzzed me on MSN chat. "We have to talk," he said. "Turn on your video."

> **For a time I forgot the ugly, the logistics; life was good—beautiful! Romance was alive!**

In the space of three minutes, he, sobbing, explained that his wife had returned begging him to take her back after an 18-month absence, and that he had to honor her request. "It's the right thing to do," he said. My head screamed, *what about me? DS? Your promises?* And my heart broke into Taps: "Day is done, gone the sun...fading light... falling night...." It broke harder than it had ever broken—not because he was the greatest love of my life (as I reflect, he was not), but because he had convinced me that I was his greatest love and that he would never ever do anything to hurt me or DS. Would I be able to trust again? How would I survive another epic rejection? Would I want to? Would I want to "subject" DS to rejection again? Would there ever be a happily ever after for us? I fell hard, and my grief was as great as having lost someone through death. My guilt too. How could I not have seen it coming? How could I have been so duped? It took a process to heal greater than I had known. As Charlie Brown noted, himself rejected time and again: *"Nothing takes the taste out of peanut butter quite like unrequited love."*[4]

One seemingly inconsequential decision to click on a dating Web site, followed by one e-mail to a married man, brought me immeasurable heartbreak and to a perceived dead-end, delaying not only my own healing and regrouping but also my son's, since until I could get myself together, I was not much help to him. It also set me back in the areas of self-esteem, and in trust. Today, I am very careful of every choice I make, no matter how small, aware that the consequences could become huge.

Consider this: You're driving and just realize you missed the turnoff, so you scoot into the right lane to turn onto the next street, without checking your rearview mirror first. Suddenly, behind you, you hear a screech, and a crash, and another crash, and another. Because you did not think things through before you decided on that last-minute move, the driver in the right lane had to slam on the brakes, which created a chain of accidents. You left a huge mess in your wake, as a result. Life is just that quirky.

 CATCH THE DRIFT: If you were to decide to explore an online single's dating site, what do you think you should consider before doing so? What is the best that can happen? What is the worst? And are you prepared for either one?

Dead-Ends, a Mirage?

Sometimes we come to what seems like a dead-end, but be aware, dead-ends are full of possibility. My friend Matt, a widower with four children, had given up hope of ever finding a woman who would accept his precious cargo of toddlers, or with whom he could trust as an exemplary co-parent. He had been online on dating Web sites, had attended singles' outings, joined singles' clubs, and even led a singles' group. Although he had plenty of dates, none measured up, and if he saw even a hint of a spark, it usually fizzled after the first "this is what your life could be like" outing with the children. One day he met a woman at the checkout of the supermarket.

He commented on a purchase she'd made of some applesauce cups. "My favorite," he said, "especially the raspberry."

"Oh, I love the mango," she said, "but these are for my son, in hospital." This launched a conversation about her child and the reasons for his hospitalization, and, as he helped her to the car with her bags, Matt briefed her on his own situation, and she shared that she was a single mother. He gave her his card, giving her the option of contacting him if she desired to take the meeting further. She called a few weeks later, they dated for a few months, and recently married and bought a new home together; the blending of the families smooth and uneventful. What an unexpected highway beyond the dead-end barrier!

> Our restricted knowledge of the future sometimes causes us to see dead-end signs where there aren't any. Life is full of possibilities, so be prepared to hurdle those obstacles when you see them.

Get a Grip on Your Expectations

To avoid burdensome regrets today, I ask myself if an expectation is realistic. Often when we are alone or lonely, particularly if we have suffered loss of a loved one in any manner, we tend to expect a lot. As a believer in God, I do tend to dream high—after all, He did create the universe. However, I do have to ensure that I divide the larger dreams and hopes into steps, so that I can celebrate achievements and modify choices and directions, if necessary. Because when I fall, I fall hard in disappointment. This minimizes future regrets and cures overanalysis, and the "it's not easy being green" blues. Because I'm happier, so is my son, and I'm that much easier to love!

Soulmate Fantasy

I grew up with childhood ideals of helpless princesses awaiting their rescues and happily-ever-afters from their princes. In my early teens, movies, television, and music introduced me to divine sublime romance. As a young adult, I dated and discovered that no one lives up to those perfect ideals, nor was I able to fit the fashioned-by-media mold, and, as a result, didn't feel I measured up, eventually deciding something must be wrong with me not to be able to attract and keep the ideal person. The soulmate fantasy[5] is just one example of an unrealistic expectation. I imagined my soulmate based on an unrealistic image engraved in my mind, and set out on a quest to find my Ken doll, and left a trail of rejection (and perhaps Mr. Right) and regret in my wake.

 CATCH THE DRIFT: What are you looking for in a person? This is an important question because if you are holding out for someone who crosses all the t's and dots all the i's on your want list, in all likelihood, you are setting yourself up for a mother lode of regret. Moreover, you may be looking for the wrong things because what you want is not necessarily what you need. This I cover in greater detail in Chapter Eight.

Permission to Be Human

I have a single mother friend, 55, who has never remarried after her divorce from Bob,[6] although she has been on a quest to find Mr. Right for 20 years. Now an empty nester, she wonders if that perfect person will ever come along. Jane[7] is a perfectionist, and she expects perfection in others, so I highly doubt it. "He's messy...he calls too much...he wore the same shirt twice...he has a joe job...he parts his hair on the wrong side...*yada*, *yada*, and *yada*." Almost every time I see her she has a dating tale of woe, is critical and faultfinding, and she wears worry like a bad wig.

> **The perfect partner Jane is searching for does not exist, but I believe the perfect person for her is out there.**

Reality is, we are not perfect, our future mates are not perfect, and we and they will fall short of our expectations. The perfect partner Jane is searching for does not exist, but I believe the perfect person for her is out there. She will find him if she stops trying to create him, stops writing his story, and starts living her own tale! Her potential significant other is a person, an individual with his own ways of doing things, his own dreams, thoughts, ideals, fears, traits, and personality. He may have things in common with her but also differences that will make him attractive, special, and complementary to her life. Only when she learns to appreciate and respect individuality and stops sweating the small stuff will she meet the perfect person for her, likely the person she least suspects would be perfect for her.

Use Your Love Eye

American philosopher Sam Keen notes: *"Love isn't finding a perfect person. It's seeing an imperfect person perfectly."*[8] To do something perfectly is to do something in love, which is the purest motivation, with patience and kindness, without envy, pride, or boastfulness, without rudeness or self-seeking motive, without anger, without keeping records of wrongs, rejoicing in the truth.[9] Love believes the best. It views another person with a keen eye of appreciation on his or her strengths and the positives, assuming and hoping the best even if in doubt. In the event two people are not a match, the love eye approach reduces the regret load of both parties, with little if any offense taken, self-esteem intact, the blow of rejection softened, and hope still alive.

 CATCH THE DRIFT: In determining if someone is right for you, do it in love and you are doing it right. The Creator of the Universe, who is Love, in creating you, designed your DNA so that the choice to function in love is the only choice that will bring you fulfillment. Truth always surfaces in love. Love brings a person's character to the top like cream for closer inspection of moral standards, virtues, and values, to help you assess the proportions of pros and cons for the best choice possible.

Lighten Up

As the title of the song goes, "Don't shoot the wounded."[10] And don't shoot yourself, either. Only when we stop convicting ourselves will we be able to give others the breaks they too deserve.

People Change

To avoid regret in your search for love, also keep the following in mind: People will change no matter how hard they try not to, and you will, too. As a person matures, each new level of growth brings different ideas, needs, and desires. Charles Dickens, as you recall in Chapter Three, may have viewed Catherine as a perfect for him at first, but as he rose in notoriety and status, she seemed quite flawed to him. The person you saw as perfect for you when you were 21 could seem quite flawed when you are 40. Love makes a choice: This is the person I wanted to know when I was 21, and this is the person I want to keep getting to know at 40, even if the shine of new love (and bouncy hair) has worn off.

Below the Surface

Date: _____

Are my children OK?

_____

_____

_____

I Beg Your Pardon, I Never Promised You a Rose Garden

What are their fears?

What do they need?

Who or what is my ultimate concern right now?

What has happened to me?

What is happening to me?

What's next?

_____

_____

What do I really want?

_____

_____

_____

_____

Why am I worried?

_____

_____

_____

_____

What am I most afraid of?

_____

_____

_____

_____

What is deep down inside of me that I haven't brought forth yet?

_____

_____

_____

_____

What do I have to offer?

_____

_____

_____

_____

What truths or lies have shaped my perceptions of me?
_____
_____
_____
_____

How faithful am I to my yearnings?
_____
_____
_____
_____

What sacrifices have I made?
_____
_____
_____
_____

Who has sacrificed for me?
_____
_____
_____
_____

What am I grateful for?
_____
_____
_____
_____

Who can I reach out to?
_____
_____
_____
_____

Who is the top person in my support network?
_____
_____
_____

Who do I need to forgive?
_____
_____
_____

Endnotes

1. Leo Buscaglia, quoted at http://www.onlylovequotes.com/miscellaneous-love-quotes/perfect-love-is-rare-indeed-for-to-be-a-lover.
2. Richard Bandler, quoted at http://theforwardcoach.org/quotes.
3. Maurice Chevalier, quoted at http://en.thinkexist.com/quotation/many_a_man_has_fallen_in_love_with_a_girl_in_a/215146.html.
4. Charles M. Schultz, Charlie Brown, "Peanuts," quoted at http://thinkexist.com/quotation/nothing_takes_the_taste_out_of_peanut_butter/228293.html.
5. Mary-Lou Galacian, *Sex, Love, and Romance in the Mass Media* (Mahwah, NJ: Lawrence Erlbaum Associates, Publishers 2004). Mary-Lou Galician describes other types of "fantasies" in her book.
6. Name changed for privacy.
7. Name changed for privacy.

8. Sam Keen, quoted at http://thinkexist.com/quotes/Sam_Keen/.
9. Paraphrase of the First Book of Corinthians, Chapter 13, in the New Testament of the Holy Bible.
10. Chuck Girard, "Don't Shoot the Wounded" (Sea of Glass Music, 1982).

Chapter Six

You Can't Date or Remarry. Not Never!
...And You Shouldn't Have...Sex?

Your Children, Your Dating, and You

Balancing romance while focusing on parental relationship and responsibility requires finesse. It is a complex situation needing great sensitivity, awareness, resolve, and patience.

You may feel ready to date, to have someone new in your life, but are your children ready for such change? Do they even know that you want to date? And, should you forgo romance if they are not ready? If divorced, our dating anyone other than the other parent is not easy for the single-parented child, young or grown, to accept because many hold out hope for the parents to get back together. This reunion fantasy is tenacious, with some children clinging to the dream even after one parent has recommitted or married. I recall as a youngster dreaming that my dad and mom would get back together, even though my dad used to beat her up. I reasoned, if they love me enough, they will. Some children of divorce resent our dating because they are being protective of the other parent's feelings, they don't want to see the other parent get hurt if there is another person in our lives, even years after a legal separation. I had an "order" from my then-eight-year-old DS "Never to marry...*not nev-errrr!*" because he wanted me all to himself. Oh, it was OK for his father to date, but not Mommy, no-sir-ee-bob, DS forbade me to ever so much as even kiss a frog.

> **Poor DS, his entire precious eight-year-old identity was very much tied to both Nathan and I.**

Poor DS, his entire precious eight-year-old identity was very much tied to both Nathan and I. When our relationship crumbled, his sense of self plummeted, and he even questioned if we loved him. He grew lonely, separated, distant, and insecure, despite my efforts to reassure him—and bossy! The little guy questioned me about weird things like, "Was I an accident, Mom, or did you really want me?" and he worried constantly about what would happen this minute or the next. I felt for him because, as a victim of a broken home myself, I had worried at times where my life was headed.[1]

As DS matured, adjusted, he became more receptive about me dating, and then it turned into:

"Mom, you're not going to wear *that* dress, to meet *him* are you?"

"What do you think I should wear?"

"Just put on your old jeans and a sweat top...and get that pink stuff off your lips...."

Hopefully, in your time of self-imposed singleness and healing, you are able to address your children's deeper concerns and anxieties because it will help free them to accept the truth, and any changes in the long run.

For the most part, our dating or remarriage cements the message that we will never reunite with their mother or father. In the case of the loss of a spouse through death, a child might feel as if we are being disloyal to the parent or his or her memory particularly, if while dating, we keep referring to ourselves as happier now than ever.

The younger ones may vocalize their thoughts, are more apt to share their feelings, though may not always be upfront because they don't want to make you sad; but the older ones, and I've seen this with DS, you see it tear up in their eyes, or if teens, in their eye rolls or shrugs; and often they just cope with it all on their own, displaying apathy, acting out their frustrations, or in becoming withdrawn or angry.

If you get weird signals when you tell your children you're ready to date, or while dating, or even entering the commitment phase, there are ways to ease their anxiety, properly and age appropriately address their concerns, and stay connected while you cultivate the romance side of your life. Whatever you do, don't keep them in the dark; address their fears head on. "Are you concerned we'll move away one day?" "Are you concerned that you won't be my number one man anymore?" "Are you feeling that your dad would be sad to know I'm dating someone?" If your child is still confused, he may need more time to heal before dealing with your dating or commitment plan. It helped DS considerably when I promised him that I would never ever marry someone who wasn't right for him, too.

 CATCH THE DRIFT: Please be aware of how dating affects your children, particularly because they have already been through so much upheaval, readjustment, and changes. Be attentive to their reactions to a new partner; not so much letting them dictate what you can and cannot do, but at least giving them a say or a chance to express their concerns, and being considerate of them. Every child is different in age and maturity level, and in how he or she has handled a family breakup or the loss of a parent. Do ensure you give your children time to process everything, being sensitive to their boundaries, and yours. This will make your dating not only more enjoyable for you but much more manageable for your children.

Only introduce or involve the children if it is to be a committed relationship. My friend Michael's daughter would become quickly attached to his new dating interests, craving a motherly presence and female companionship. As a result, every time a relationship ended, Tilly felt a sense of deep loss. Breakups are confusing and upsetting for children; constant breakups even worse, so it's best not to introduce the children to a new love interest unless entering into a serious commitment with the intent of marriage. Children don't understand the intricacies and highs and lows of adult relationship, most don't have the emotional maturity to process it all.

When the conditions are right, keep the introduction informal and friendly. Meet at a park or the beach or for hotdogs; someplace fun. Don't expect instant acceptance but do expect manners. A child might act jealous, hostile, or shy. Give the relationship time; it's natural, and does not necessarily mean "not never!"

In an age-appropriate way, encourage their openness. Don't solicit their approval or try to manipulate your children to like your partner but do be there to listen and to answer their questions. Avoid, "See? I told you she was not Godzilla and wouldn't bite your head off." Emphasize in love and deed your continued unconditional love and commitment to your child, never breaking your personal dates with your son or daughter, making more if necessary, and always keeping your promises.

Resist going into "Instant Family" mode. Don't bring your partner along on every family outing; transition into it gradually. If your partner has children, they too will appreciate a slower transition. Don't force the children together, or force their relationships with one another. This will create jealousy and animosity! Spend regular alone time with your children, and encourage your partner to do the same with his or her children. This sends the message to your children that they are still vital to you, that you love being around them, and that their thoughts and opinions and feelings are still important to you.

Before you transition from dating to a long-term commitment, evaluate your child's thoughts, your relationship, and your partner to determine if she or he is right for your child, for your family. Some things to consider:

- Have you any hesitations at all?
- What concerns does your child have about your relationship with your partner?
- Has your child met this person? If so, is your child comfortable with him or her?
- If your partner is a single parent, how active a role does he or she play? Are the child support payments up to date?
- How does he or she talk about the ex, about your ex or previous spouse?
- Has he or she breached or overstepped boundaries with your children?
- Does your child enjoy when he or she visits?

- Does he or she appear to enjoy spending time with your child?

- Do you know how your love interest deals in testing: under stress, disappointment, anger?

- Have you included your child on some of your outings or dates?

- Does he or she mind if you and your child do things by yourself?

- In an argument, does he or she fight fair, refraining from physical, verbal, or emotional abuse?

- Do you respect this person?

- If you have introduced your love interest to your extended family and friends, did they like him or her?

- Can this person support him or herself? Does the person have his or her own home?

- Are you still having as much one-on-one time with your child as you did before?

- Has this person seen how you parent, in all situations? Did he or she agree, disagree?

- Have you established boundaries regarding physical intimacy in front of the children? Has he or she agreed?

- Have you both discussed future plans together, your expectations?

Set appropriate boundaries around sexual displays of affection in front of the children. Our children look to us as role models. Sleepovers send the message that sexual intimacy before marriage is OK. As a result of desiring my son to remain pure before marriage, overnights never happened. Controlled physical displays of affection in front of your children with someone you've known for a while, someone they have at least somewhat accepted into their lives (such as light and occasional kissing, hand holding, hugs) can, however, send a positive message to the children. This brings me to a delicate subject: sex before remarriage.

Now this might cause you to put down the book, but please read on, with an open mind, because what I have to say is important. Of course, the decision is yours, but I have to speak my heart on this matter.

Because I had been married before, for some reason men thought it was OK for me to have sex outside of marriage. After all, I was no longer "pure." But more than ever, I was determined to remain pure until I remarried, because of personal conviction, yes, because of health risks, yes, but also because I wanted to set an example for DS!

Every year, millions of new sexually transmitted disease infections occur in the United States and Canada;

potentially hundred of millions occurrences globally. HIV/AIDS (acquired immune deficiency syndrome), gonorrhea, syphilis, herpes, chlamydia, vaginitis, hepatitis, pubic lice (ugh) and crabs (ugh-ugh), mononucleosis. The chances of contracting some of these diseases are high, clothes on or off!

Let me ask you: How well do you think you could parent if you had nerve or brain damage? If you were blind? How devastating would it be to you to learn that you only have a year to live, and that your death would be slow and painful, whereby your body would waste away to nothing before your children's eyes. What if you passed on a disease to your child? What if you want more children one day, but were suddenly told, "Sorry, you're infertile." These are all risks associated with sexual promiscuity, so please think long and hard before entering into physical intimacy outside of marriage.

Why, why, why, would we as parents take such risk? Why would we, as self-respecting human beings, take such a chance? And why would we want to expose our children, or encourage them that sex outside of marriage is OK? Don't get me wrong, I'm not a prude, nor am I "old fashioned," but we need to keep to our high standards if we are to expect our children to adhere to them. Actually, "purity" while single is a growing trend in North America, and no wonder. Who wants to be married to someone who smells fishy, with blisters and warts in his or her private parts, who would risk laying with someone who could potentially kill him or her? Do you know how many millions of bacteria are exchanged in just one deep kiss?

I see so many single parents doing a brilliant job of protecting their children, except in this one area. It's not enough to teach safe sex. We have to teach no sex before marriage. It starts with us. We really have to guard the gates here. Sex is so wonderful in sanctified love. Our modeling abstinence while single will create safeguards, not guarantees, that our children will wait, and a better chance of their remaining pure, and with dignity and self-respect intact.

Anything outside of the marriage bed is counterfeit sex. It is not the way it was meant to be—this worry about disease, unwed pregnancies, rejections. The best sex in the world is the kind you don't have to be sorry for, the kind that doesn't say, "By the way, what's your name?" The kind that knows exactly where to touch, that allows you to be selfish in your need of it. The kind that isn't filled with heartbreaks and breakups, that rolls over in the morning to a familiar and comforting face that whispers your name. The kind of sex without inhibition, full of variety, without shame, and looking forward to familiar tastes. The kind of sex that doesn't have to tiptoe down the hall and out the door afterward....

Every person we have sex with has the potential to become an ex. We don't need more exes! Before you roll in the hay, ask yourself, is it really worth it? And if you're feeling pressured or threatened by breakup or made to feel guilty about abstaining, count it as the other person's serious flaw, and run. It might be for your life.

It will take some planning, and another look at your core values and regrets to form resolve and strategy to prevent regrets and more importantly, to save yourself for the one meant for you.

Below the Surface

Date: _____

Are my children OK?
_____
_____
_____
_____

What are their fears?
_____
_____
_____
_____

What do they need?
_____
_____
_____
_____

Who or what is my ultimate concern right now?
_____
_____
_____
_____

What has happened to me?
_____
_____
_____
_____

What is happening to me?

What's next?

What do I really want?

Why am I worried?

What am I most afraid of?

What is deep down inside of me that I haven't brought forth yet?

You Can't Date or Remarry. Not Never!...And You Shouldn't Have...Sex?

What do I have to offer?

What truths or lies have shaped my perceptions of me?

How faithful am I to my yearnings?

What sacrifices have I made?

Who has sacrificed for me?

What am I grateful for?

Who can I reach out to?

Who is the top person in my support network?

Who do I need to forgive?

Endnote

1. In *The Single Parent's Guide to Raising Godly Children* (Shippensburg, PA: Destiny Image, 2010), I address at length ways to boost your child's sense of security.

Chapter Seven

Do Flowers in Spring Say, "Not Yet"?[1]

How to See, Find, and Fit the Right Person Into Your Life

"All the windows of my heart I open to the day."
—John Greenleaf Whittier[2]

When you hear the word *fulfillment,* what do you imagine? Only you know, from within the deepest places of your heart, what a fulfilled life looks like—and don't be surprised if you cannot articulate some things because the greater depths of fulfillment can only be articulated by the heart.[3] For me, and I'm generalizing here, fulfillment is to have someone to love and to have someone love me, to have something to do and someone to help, and to have something to hope for.

Using Your Heart to See and Find Your Perfect Match

Most of us are familiar with the five senses: touch, smell, taste, sound, and sight. But do you know that your heart is a sense? And, it is highly underused! *"Teach us to number our days, that we may gain a heart of wisdom."*[4] Life is precious, and each day valuable. Every action, thought, moment, counts. To ensure we maximize the potential of each day, we have to apply our hearts to wisdom—that is, use the eyes of our heart to steer us to what will really fulfill us, not what we perceive will fill us. In searching for a belle or beau, a wise heart will lead us to the best person for us, someone who will help fulfill needs we have perhaps yet to perceive, because the heart is the seat of our emotions, our values, our spirit, and our beliefs, the core of who we are. The head will prod us toward the candy, a wise heart will steer us toward things truly good for us, genuine sustenance. The head may tell us we'll never meet the right person. The heart convinces us, he or she is out there.

The inability to see with the eyes of the heart will cause us to lose heart, and if that happens, our dreams will die because the heart fuels the spirit. When our dreams die, so does a part of us die. I would rather lose my physical eyesight than to lose heart.

You've come this far in *The Single Parent's Guide to Love, Dating, and Relationships*, and by now you've had opportunity to look inward, to examine your core values, to heal and to rise in faith to believe in the greatest outcomes for you and family. Or at least I have you thinking about it. Perhaps now you can see more clearly with the eyes of your heart what it is you and your family truly need. If that need is someone new in your lives, you'll have a clearer picture of who that person is. Set that someone on a foundation of your core values, standards, and beliefs. Then, put some action into it by creating a plan or strategy to find him or her because fulfillment is a way of travel, not a destination.[5] It is an expression of the heart in considered action.[6] It is something we carry out, bring into effect or actuality in our search.

> CATCH THE DRIFT: Considering your core values, standards, and beliefs, what fills you up? What can another person give you that you cannot give to yourself? What brings you joy? While you're at it, don't forget about your child's physical, emotional, spiritual, and material needs. Sort it all out. Weigh and define everything in order of importance. Sincerely, take time to do this because it is a method of keeping things in perspective and at the forefront in the event your heart does grow sick. We have a better chance of reaping wisely if we do not lose heart!

For a time, my search for love was head-based according to my headspace. I was searching for someone to rescue me because I was scared. I searched for someone to fill a hole because I felt incapable. But this either attracted the God's-gift-to-women or the controller types, consequently setting those relationships up for failure. Additionally, even if they were sound people, expecting them to be solely responsible for boosting my self-esteem, lessening my feelings of insecurity, allaying fears, or bringing me a peace of mind, would have placed great demands on them because ultimately my happiness and peace of mind was my responsibility. My head wouldn't tell me that, of course. However, when I used my heart as a lantern, I could better define how someone might help, enhance, or come alongside of me in my areas of need or perceived needs: the needs of intimacy, respect, love, honor; the needs to be loved, honored, heard, cherished, protected. Who am I kidding, I just wanted to be held!

If you just cannot dig deep enough in your own heart to see, survey the hearts of the people already in your life or in the past: family members or friends who brought out the best in you, left you feeling full of life, safe, comfortable, and emotionally healthy! Think about those who have been kind, patient, attentive, long-suffering, with you, with your child. Think about the listeners, and those who have prayed for you, held your hand, loved on you unconditionally. Think about those you are most comfortable with; where you can be your true self and they only love you more. These are the traits to look for in a love interest. These are the things that you need and deserve!

Try this: The greatest way to spot a counterfeit is to study the real deal! Create a profile of your future love interest, listing the qualities important to you, and you'll recognize a poseur before you can say, "Two mocha double lattes, please."

Ding! Ding! Your desperation or fear may turn *you* into the poseur playing the role of someone you are not, to impress. The worst thing that can happen is to not be yourself. Study yourself so that you can spot when you're trying to fake it to make something happen. Create your own profile or CV, listing your qualities, giftings, talents, values, assets, plans, aspirations, limits, limitations, and the things important to you.

Remember: Be true to yourself.

Use Your Heart to See Why

Looking through the lens of the heart will also help you decide why you want to date. You might discover it is for all the wrong reasons. Loneliness alone isn't a good enough reason to get serious with someone—you are looking for someone to share your life with, not to fill a gap. Please don't set yourself up to handle more than you currently can emotionally. Such heartache wasn't what I needed when Navy Man suddenly pulled the plug on our relationship, which was built on the foundation of my loneliness. Sometimes all I needed was a hand to hold, and a heart to understand, or a friend like Jim Carrey to act goofy with in the throes of grief. You might discover your reason is simply because you are bored or need social contact. Again, wrong reasons to want to settle down with someone. Your heart may help you see that you are still too emotionally raw. Big life changes can further sap our reserves, so decide now not to jump into the first relationship that comes along—you may not yet have the judgment to see your date's flaws. Also, consider that your children will greatly influence your reasons, your readiness, and your willingness to begin a new relationship.

> Sometimes all I needed was a hand to hold, and a heart to understand.

 CATCH THE DRIFT: Identify as many elements as you can based on your vision of the right person for you. Will your future love have a specific personality type? Is humor important? Honesty? Take it further. Does she have plans? A good work ethic? Is he responsible? Yearnings, things that draw you, things that satisfy, things that you love, may help you to identify more elements.

Once you've written everything down, put some zip into it by setting it on a foundation of your core values; then create a plan or strategy to get what you need. Remember, fulfillment is a way of travel.... What do you have to do to meet someone? Where do you have to go? Whom do you know who might know such people? What days do you have available? How much do you have to set aside for a babysitter? If you don't have excess money to spend, how can you make more? Who in your family might take care of the children a few hours a week?

Creating such a plan will give you clarity, and always take you back to the heart of the matter if your head misdirects you.

> CATCH THE DRIFT: Assess what you have to offer. Your self-esteem may have taken a few hits, so don't quit writing until you list at least 10, preferably 20 or more qualities, gifts, and abilities that you can offer to someone special. If you are having difficulty, ask your family, close friends, and coworkers. Be clear to yourself about where you are right now, where your kids are, and what you want and they need. Be sure of your motives, and you'll have the courage to state those motives on the first date: "I am not ready to get serious." "I'm looking for my soulmate."

Making Room for Love

My dating life as a single parent was a scheduling nightmare and often left me wondering if there really was any time for romance while raising my son, who took top priority. Call me *romantically challenged*! We had little enough time together, with DS at school, my work, and his time at his dad's, so I cherished and maximized every moment we had together. Especially at first, when he was still so tender, I didn't want to be away from him for a second, and didn't want to upset the balance I'd recreated, nor did I want too many new intrusions! Thus my tee-up plans for dates went something like this:

"The soonest I can fit you in, Bobby, would be, say, for an hour 3.5 weeks from Tuesday, at 6:00 a.m. That's assuming, of course, that my son is over the chicken pox, because he doesn't like to be sick at his father's, and if I finish my manuscript by then. Starbucks on Clarke Road, OK?"

Poor Bobby would be traveling 2,000 miles for a 60-minute date with an already overstressed blonde.

Eventually, I did sort out my time better, settled DS in the new routines, and did make room for love, but it wasn't easy! Bobby and I worked on a once-a-month plan, with him coming here if I could not get away.

Starting out again was not easy. I didn't know where to even meet men, never mind the type of man I needed. Oh, I'd seen plenty of single men at Safeway, but I was always more focused on picking up the pogo sticks than I was on bagging a guy. If anything, though, single parenthood wized me to what I didn't want and alerted me to the small, daily happenings that make life so spectacular even single. And I thank the Lord for not giving me everything in life that I asked for. Life always has and will be like a roll of toilet paper; the closer to the end I get, the faster life goes. So, not being a spring chicken, I felt an urgency, no pun intended.

I found Bobby from home, on an online dating site. Networking for dates this way has its pluses and minuses, the downside being that most of the men I met online lived far away, the plus being I could prospect at night, when my son was asleep. Getting together with someone who lives far away is a real trip, and I mean that quite literally. It's not like we can just meet up for a walk on the seawall; it takes planning, finances, and time—the latter two I could ill afford. Hence, the onus was always on the man to get here for the first date. Usually, the first ~~five~~ 23 or so dates, mostly because I hated to be far away from DS.

> "If you ever get a second chance in life for something, you've got to go all the way."
> —LANCE ARMSTRONG

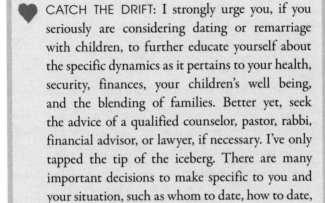

CATCH THE DRIFT: I strongly urge you, if you seriously are considering dating or remarriage with children, to further educate yourself about the specific dynamics as it pertains to your health, security, finances, your children's well being, and the blending of families. Better yet, seek the advice of a qualified counselor, pastor, rabbi, financial advisor, or lawyer, if necessary. I've only tapped the tip of the iceberg. There are many important decisions to make specific to you and your situation, such as whom to date, how to date, the complexity of exes, legalities, what stage of transition you are in, and whether a relationship will best meet and serve the needs of everyone involved. An ounce of prevention is worth a pound of cure, and armed with knowledge, you are safeguarding your family.

Romance has a way of keeping us fresh, young, energized, and alive. Falling in love made me want to be a better person. And while for many single parents the definition of romance might not be what it once was—the consuming passion of youth perhaps—it can still be exciting, ultraromantic, and highly fun and informative, as long as you remember to respect yourself and your children, being especially careful where they are concerned. Dating can be a good experience—and if you make time for it, it might just bring you a new and wonderful forever partner and welcome household addition.

No Time for Love?

Nurturing, growing, and keeping a relationship flourishing takes time, which is a precious commodity for many of us pressured by the demands on our time: children, household chores, work, finances, extended family obligations. But by establishing priorities and setting goals, by making better use of the time we have, and by creating time we don't think we have, we can find more time for dating and relationship.

There are ways in which to capitalize on the time that we do have to either search out prospects, go out on quality dates, or maximize time with a romantic partner without compromising our quality time with the children.

It may take analysis and scheduling shifting. Single dad Cameron, a neighbor with two children under ten, prefers to be home in the evenings with his daughters. This is their quality time together. To accommodate romance, because he has a flexible job, he shifts dates to earlier hours: breakfast, midmorning coffees, movie matinees. Two Saturdays a month, when the children are with their mother, he reserves for dinners or special events. Kathy, on the other hand, a widow with four children, doesn't have the luxury of flexible hours, so she keeps her eyes open for single dads who understand her situation better than single men without children do. Often, their dates are on the go, at their children's soccer practices, while volunteering on field trips, or grocery shopping rendezvous.

Margaret and Pete planned one specific night a week for their date. She traded daily childcare time with her neighbor friend.

In my time analysis, I had to separate what was extremely important from what was not as important. In other words, vital versus not so vital. For a parent, this should be a no brainer, but sometimes stress or fatigue blurred the line between the two categories, so it really helped me to prioritize and free up some hours. Of course, things like getting my son off to school, helping him with his homework, spending time chatting together, going places, was important. Work was vital—I had to earn a living. But watching the latest episode of *The Bachelor,* or washing the kitchen floor four times a month, or spending two hours a week getting my nails done, or ironing DS's underwear, could be classified as not so vital, depending on my mindset! By eliminating a few things, I freed up some time to spend with my honey.

Surmounting Common SP Obstacles

Single parents definitely are presented with unique obstacles but most are not insurmountable. We may have to hire babysitters, which is costly, and worrisome; and we can only rely on friends and family to a point, bless their precious hearts. We also have built-in roomies to consider: our children! Thus, we won't be inviting our dates home for a cozy dinner for two for eons. Nor can we stay out late. The babysitter has to be taken home, Nana needs her rest. If you are a single dad, likely you'll be doing more of the spending on a date, and this may eat into your budget. We also have to plan our social outings well in advance to make the appropriate arrangements, or to save up for the date, so rarely is meeting someone new a spur-of-the-moment decision. You may still also have some loose ends to tie up: financial, custody, estate settling, insurance issues, and other legal matters.

All single parents are package deals. We come with exes: Ex-spouse, ex-inlaws, perhaps ex-friends, and a little more emotional baggage. Finding good prospects who love children, more particularly, with the potential of loving your children, further narrows your choices.

In addition, you have to consider if the person is a good fit for the children, and whether your children are ready. Has your child built a new relationship with you yet if you are the only parent involved in his life? Dating too soon may cheat your child of her time with you. Plus, you want to ensure you are safe because your family depends on you, and taking chances to date is not wise. Ever. But there are ways to get over the humps, in finding prospects, and in safely and healthfully managing the relationships according to my savvy dating single parent friends:

Take a good look in the mirror. With all you've been through, you may have let yourself go a little (or a lot), or perhaps you might be a little out of date. Explore the malls, magazines, current fashion trends for your age group, and decide if you need to add a new fresh look to your wardrobe. Visit the barber or your hair stylist, and ask how best to update your look, perhaps a way to wear your hair up, or a cut that will make you feel new. Perhaps shave off the moustache (especially if you're a girl!). Do you need to gain weight? Don't laugh, I lost much weight through stress. Do you need to lose weight? Are you out of shape? Start an exercise and nutrition program, walk every day, eat the right foods, and shine inside and out.

Prospecting…

Singles Groups. Some cities have Parents Without Partners groups more for support and group activities than for dating. Still though, you are meeting people whose lives are similar to yours with the same challenges. And it's an opportunity to network.

Online. Although I'm not big on the personal dating sites, from experience, and won't recommend any here, love connections do happen that way. However, be sure to do your homework, and don't offer too much information. Definitely never post a photo of yourself with your children. And definitely don't post a photo of yourself in which it is obvious that you've cut out your ex, the one that shows an arm around you but no body to go with it.

Network Through Trusted Sources. Meet new people through your good friends, or family members who already know you and your situation.

SP Hangouts. Look around you. Likely, you are frequenting places where other single parents are: at ball games, music practices, fast food joints.

Avoid bars. Enough said.

Avoid reality television shows. Enough said.

Avoid dark alleys, bridges. Enough said.

Avoid prisons. Enough said.

First Few Dates

Your safety. Always be sure someone close to you knows where you are going and with whom. Let that person know when you'll be home, and take your cell phone with you in case of an emergency. Let your date know tactfully that someone knows your whereabouts or about your meeting and that you might get a call.

Make it short. If you share custody, plan dates when your child is with the other parent, or when the child is busy. If you are meeting someone for the first time face-to-face, in person (and I'm trusting you've done a background check on him or her, and that you have informed a trusted friend or family member of your plans to meet this person), meet for half an hour or so while your child is at a birthday party or game, way out of sight and earshot of your child! If you like the person, you can schedule in another date; if not, you have an excuse to leave.

Go to a busy public place. Your personal safety is important. Go somewhere where you are not dependent on the person for a lift home.

Keep it low key. Look for places that encourage conversation and interaction, such as a walk in a public area or a quieter coffee shop, a place to get to know each other. Movies aren't good for this.

Don't force the issue. Don't try to convince someone to be comfortable about the fact that you have children. And don't hide it. Your mission is to find someone who will not only embrace you but your family as well.

Get your story straight. Your date may get personal, but details are not necessary. Decide on a short, nonjudgmental, nonscathing explanation. He or she does not need the nitty gritty of the separation, loss, divorce, or abandonment; be brief, move on. If you can't talk about it without being angry, accusatory, overly tearful, or vengeful, you are definitely not ready for another relationship. Generalize about your children if asked (such as ages, interests, goals). Again, don't provide any personal information concerning them (such as names of schools or sports teams); shield them at this stage.

Get caught up on current events. It might help to discuss current events as pregnant pause fillers.

Ask your date open-ended questions that motivate more than a yes or no response. Ask about the person's interests, dreams, goals; this is flattering and says to the person that you are a great listener and someone to consider spending more time with.

Relationship Building 101

"I'm thinking of you and want to be with you." Say it with flowers picked on the side of the road, love letters, use

of Internet and telephone (using speaker or headset) for chats, meeting for lunch while the children are at school, small surprise gifts.

Share the little things together, not just the big news. Focus on the other person, ask open-ended questions, and listen.

Find one sure time to "see" each other every week at the very least, whether in person or through video chat, and don't break the date. Have a back-up plan just in case. Change it up once in a while if you can from evenings to days and days to evenings.

Take turns planning activities—surprise each other. You can be generous without spending money. Prepare a picnic, discover a new bike ride route, go to garage sales, go to open houses, whatever it is—just make it special, rather than ho-hum.

Commute to work together, or plan for early morning coffee or meet for lunch. Rendezvous after work for a walk in a park.

Keep the home fires burning. The local diner or family restaurant may not be posh but there's something about meeting over old-fashioned homestyle food that brings comfort and easiness to the relationship.

Keep the romance alive. Conversely, meeting at a place with chi-chi can also have good romantic effect and aftereffect.

Share and reenergize. Ball games or sporting events are a great way to reenergize together as a couple. The adrenaline rush of a goal can bring you together in a celebratory hug, laughter, and even heartbreak for a loss, revitalizing the chemistry between you.

Evaluate the Heart of the Relationship

- Are the children getting enough time with me?

- Are their emotional/physical/spiritual needs being met?

- Do I feel smothered? Not paid attention to?

- Am I more loved or loving?

- Can I live with his or her faults?

- Are we authentic with each other?

- Have I lost "me" somewhere?

- How frequent are the mentions of breakup?

- Are we bored with each other?

- Have we reneged on promises to each other?

- Do we both communicate well (share our hearts/listen)?
- Do I love him or her more as a brother/sister/father/child/sugarmomma or poppa?

Below the Surface

Date: _____

Are my children OK?
_____
_____
_____
_____

What are their fears?
_____
_____
_____
_____

What do they need?
_____
_____
_____
_____

Who or what is my ultimate concern right now?
_____
_____
_____

What has happened to me?

What is happening to me?

What's next?

What do I really want?

Why am I worried?

What am I most afraid of?

What is deep down inside of me that I haven't brought forth yet?

What do I have to offer?

What truths or lies have shaped my perceptions of me?

How faithful am I to my yearnings?

What sacrifices have I made?

Who has sacrificed for me?
___

What am I grateful for?
___

Who can I reach out to?
___

Who is the top person in my support network?
___

Who do I need to forgive?
___

Endnotes

1. From a quote by Norman Douglas: "Why always 'not yet'? Do flowers in spring say, 'not yet'"? Quoted at http://www

.famousquotesandauthors.com/authors/norman_douglas_quotes.html.

2. John Greenleaf Whittier, "My Psalm" (1859); accessed at http://www.readbookonline.net/readOnLine/7933/.

3. Inspired by Martin Luther King Jr.'s quote: "Occasionally in life there are those moments of unutterable fulfillment that cannot be completely explained by those symbols called words. Their meanings can only be articulated by the heart." Quoted at http://thinkexist.com/quotation/occasionally_in_life_there_are_those_moments_of/324620.html.

4. This is a quote of 120-year-old or so Moses, found in the Holy Bible, Old Testament, Book of Psalms, Chapter 90, Verse 12. He'd already lived about 43,000 days when he asked God to teach him to number them. Here he was asking God to help him count days in the right way so that he could live in the right way. He was concerned for his people, and I surmise for himself, because their hearts were hardening as they daily watched thousands of their people die. They were getting used to it. Death wasn't as much of a shock anymore. Perhaps their dreams of the Promised Land were dying, too. Seeing through the eyes of our heart is wise because even when everything around us crumbles, we don't lose sight of hope, the preciousness and vibrancy of life; and we aren't in danger of hardening, of losing the capacity to love or to feel loved.

5. Modified from a quote by Roy M. Goodman: "Remember that happiness is a way of travel—not a destination." Quoted at http://www.quotationspage.com/quotes/Roy_M._Goodman.

6. Modified from a quote by Aristotle: "Happiness is an expression of the soul in considered actions." Quoted at http://en.thinkexist.com/quotation/happiness_is_an_expression_of_the_soul_in/154750.html.

Chapter Eight

Bad Boys, Bad Girls, Whatcha Gonna Do?

(Whatcha Gonna Do When They Come for You?)

The only nuts we should entertain are those that come wrapped in chocolate, preferably almonds.

Having harnessed the good within regrets and fears, having chosen to learn more about your worth in your self-imposed period of singleness, having checked that your children are OK and more or less ready for you to sow some oats, you have hopefully grown wiser, stronger, more confident, and of firmer resolve not to repeat a mistake, not to make a poor selection or less than best decisions for you and your family.

Understanding these things and how they operate in your life should give you an idea of the type of person best for you and help you establish a level of control over who you meet, since the people you deserve are not always who you will attract. Now you have the control (hopefully) having made positive new changes that will attract your soulmate, potentially a selection of candidates, emotionally healthy ones, and within the selection, the exact right one for you and for your family. Likely, you have the wisdom and ability now not to reestablish old negative patterns that will scare the good ones away!

Imagine How Much Deeper the Ocean Without Sponges...

> "Love is fire. But whether it's gonna warm your heart or burn your house down you can never tell."
>
> —Jason Jordan[1]

Single parents are more vulnerable to scum: users, poseurs, predators, takers, losers, cheaters, abusers, narcissists, liars, deadbeats, serial daters, misandrists, misogynists, and misanthropes.[2] And if you don't believe me, tune into the television talk shows. Featured guests are usually single mothers or dads dealing with the most bizarre and heartbreaking (mostly to the kids) behaviors and situations involving boyfriends or girlfriends. This is *one reason* it *is* important to deal with the junk in the trunk—so that you and your family do not become easy targets or future guests on Springer, Povitch, Oprah, or Dr. Phil.

Don't Settle!

> "If you're going through hell, keep going."
> —Sir Winston Churchill

Commitment is not for everybody, and there are some sharks out there waiting to bite with ulterior motives: to find a sugarmomma or daddy, to score, carve another notch in the bedpost—you catch the choppy drift. Regret-filled romances are often the result of our neediness, fears, circumstances, and insecurities influencing long-term decisions. If you feel like used goods, in the manner of "I'll be lucky if anyone wants me," you are in danger of settling your heart for second best when it comes to a marriage proposal.

I latched onto the Navy Man precisely because he was the first person after my breakup who said I was beautiful, and I needed to hear it because I felt like Ugly Betty having gone through so much stress and heartbreak. If you are too needy, you are in danger of overlooking someone's potentially serious faults in your quest to fulfill what you perceive to be your greatest needs. If you have an unhealthy need to control, you might attract a clingy weakling. If you are too desperate for love, you might settle for a man who would be a better husband than he would a father, or a woman who would be a better wife than a mother.

Please do not settle! Whether you are a single parent out of wedlock, divorced, or widowed, you deserve someone with every quality important to you and your children. A model father is one who also openly demonstrates and shows his children how much he respects, loves, and cherishes their mother. The best mother is one who also models similar commitment. It is worth the wait for the right person deserving of you and your family. You *owe it* to your children whether at home or not, youngsters or adults, not to settle for second best. The sooner you fold your cards and walk away from a shady game, the better.

It Won't Be Easy, But It's Worth It

But that isn't always easy in a whirlwind courtship, when infatuated, or in a "love at first sight" scenario where we are cloud nine-ing on how the other person makes us feel rather than on who that person is. It's especially easy for the single parent to accept the first person who comes along and pays enough attention to us! I did with Navy Man, who made me feel cherished and beautiful, and heck, who are we kidding, emotionally and physically a-l-i-v-e! The fantasy in that, of course, was that I would be living on this euphoric high forever. So my thinking was, *he really must be the "right guy."* Our chemistry had very little to do at first with his character; I was caught up more in the seduction and infatuation phase, which included unrealistic promises that he could never deliver. High emotions dulled my sensibilities and perceptive senses of him. I overlooked things that would normally be cause for alarm: breaches of my core values, barriers to long-desired plans, and negative qualities that might one day devastate me and DS again—things I could not immediately see. It's hard to determine in such cases if you are truly interested in the person or if you are responding to his or her interest in you, but it can all be sorted out by staying within certain boundaries.

How to See Through a Love Haze

Connect With Your Core Values

> "Love is blind but marriage is an eye-opener."[3]

Understanding and defining our personal core values, standards, and beliefs and vowing to ourselves never to compromise them may ground us more effectively when love threatens to blind us. Core values are just that—the heart of who we are; central to our character, usually our own parents' or guardians' tenets for life modeled and taught to us as children; and in the absence of good parental modeling or in addition, they may comprise values we learned from people of influence in our childhood: teachers, coaches, pastors, or daycare givers, for example. These are things we grew up believing, embracing, and living by. Perhaps in adulthood these principles were fine-tuned or added to for a custom fit, but they are usually constant and fitting into our lives through changes and challenges, good and bad. They differ for people, of course; but root values influence our desires, tastes, and preferences; our social, moral, political, and spiritual views and interactions. Hopefully, you have healthy values!

How I wish I had been wiser and more tuned in, especially when the outwardly perfect Ken dolls came along and my heart kinda flew outta my head. I mean, how flattering that *he* would want *me!* In those instances, in the throes of infatuation, I treated my mind as a jealous friend bent on raining on my heart's parade.

He's not as into you as you think...

But...he's gorgeous, a ten!

He swears a blue streak....

It's OK, he's a little rough around the edges, so what?

He's been married 28 times...

Ya, but I could be the one...

He only wants one thing...

He's not like that, he'll wait.

Ya, for like a week—two, maybe...

Not!

Finally connecting—understanding and defining—my core values helped me discover my true needs, goals, and desires, and consequently, juxtaposed beside my own, I could recognize incompatibility sooner than later, even through the thickest love haze. Moreover, it resulted in a quicker return to logic and consequently, the resolve to heed the genuine red flags before things went too far.

> After a quarrel, a wife said to her husband, "You know, I was a fool when I married you." The husband replied, "Yes, dear, but I was in love and didn't notice."

Only Fools Rush In

Time or a search on the Internet eventually has a way of revealing serious flaws or exposing impostors. Truth will bring us out of the dream closet, for better or for worse—but do you really want to take the risk? Too much is at stake to be going for a test drive with someone who compromises your values: your children, your peace of mind, your bank roll, your self-esteem, your plans, your dreams. Cut it short, make it a deal breaker.

After four years in a long-distance relationship with and engagement to Bobby, I broke it off. Why? Because I discovered things that did not align with my values, and this made me uncomfortable. Had I missed more? Apparently, I had. In truth, thinking back, there were red flags in the beginning that I had missed, as well as areas in which I compromised. Perhaps he had similar flags. But that was four years on a journey that prevented me from potentially meeting my Mr. Right.

Every parent hoping to remarry should create a list of deal makers and deal breakers; absolute and immediately disqualifying qualities, values, and desires. Thinking about your child, your core values, your needs, your plans, your dreams, your likes and dislikes, create two checklists. One a list of must haves in a relationship, the other a scissor list—the deal breakers—absolute, immediate grounds for cutting loose from or disqualifying someone. Here's a small sampling from my own list of marriage qualifiers and "I'm outta heres." If you're a single dad, remember, I'm a girly girl, and your list may look entirely different.

Great Prospect List

- ☐ Must love/desire children
- ☐ A father's heart

> **Great Prospect List**
> ☐ Prefers to "wait"
> ☐ Similar religious beliefs
> ☐ Strong work ethics
> ☐ Financially stable/responsible
> ☐ A history of commitment
> ☐ Tender, kind-hearted
> ☐ Assertive
> ☐ Forgiving
> ☐ Attentive
> ☐ Vision
> ☐ Knows what he wants
> ☐ Sense of humor (clean)
> ☐ Wise
> ☐ Relatively handsome/in shape

Hint: Create a BONUS List. Close your eyes again and imagine in Technicolor! These are things you can live without but would be icing on the cake. You've probably already had much practice. Some call it fantasy, but really, why not believe for all that you want in a man or a woman? You know: Brown hair, blue eyes, long eyelashes, nice figure (I'm speaking for you guys here!), a guy who loves to shop, a gal who's into sports, someone who loves to give foot rubs, has a villa in Spain, you catch the drift!

> **Shae-ism:** Sometimes the only obstacle keeping us from our dreams is the fact that we don't have any!

"I'm Outta Here" List

- ☐ Physically or verbally abusive
- ☐ Deadbeat father
- ☐ Talks poorly of his ex-wife/women
- ☐ Dirty, stinky, smelly
- ☐ Aggressive
- ☐ Lying/dishonesty
- ☐ Excessive drinking/smoking
- ☐ Abusing drugs
- ☐ Addicted to porn
- ☐ Constantly ogling women
- ☐ Entitlement mindset
- ☐ Always has to be right
- ☐ Lack of goals, plans
- ☐ Pressures for sex too early
- ☐ Complains of work
- ☐ Frivolous
- ☐ Bad toupee, combover (just kidding)

Give the Truth Time to Rise

Following my heartbreak with Bobby, if I met someone and his values at first seemed to align, still I wouldn't go "exclusive" or even think about introducing him to anyone unless I continued to like what I saw as the relationship progressed, giving it a few months before committing to going steady, and only if my original checkmarks were still there (bonus if there were more) and I had not compromised in any area concerning my values statement.

Even after going steady for a few months, I constantly reassessed, and if after about six months or so, a love interest stuck to his original guns, and me mine, only then would I consider introducing him to friends, family, and DS. If not, I severed the tie. Cut my losses. Scrammed. Vamoosed. More often than not. That is why I've become a philosopher! On that note and in retrospect, all of my failed relationships were in some way related to or the result of core value incompatibility.

If you are currently in an "iffy" dating relationship: I encourage you to take a hard, tough look at your current love interest and ask yourself if he or she aligns with your values. Is she still patient? Does he trust me? How has he changed? Is she still the same person? Does he have an even character? Is she double-minded? Is he lazy? Is she cheap? Does he resent the children? Does he like me for me, or does he constantly try to change me? Is she secretive? Nuts? Have I uncovered untruths? Am I trying to change her? Does he assume the right to control how I live and behave? Is she charming one moment, angry the next? Does he belittle my feelings, accomplishments, faith? Does she blame me for all that goes wrong in the relationship? Is he jealous? Am I always apologizing?

If something doesn't seem right but you cannot pinpoint what it is, trust your instinct. Many of these questions may reveal a disturbing pattern of emotional unbalance. But before you conclude anything, take a hard, tough look at *you*; determine that it is not an old relationship pattern of insecurities or fears making you feel uneasy. Understandably, relationships take work, but they should also be pleasing and peaceful. If something in his or her character raises an alarm, heed it. If it's your problem, definitely acknowledge it or take necessary steps to overcome it.

Caveat: My girlfriend Marie suffers deep bouts of depression. She is bipolar, but her boyfriend of six months is unaware of this, and is constantly left wondering why at times she seems so distant, ignoring his calls, lashing back at him for no reason, or treating him badly. Although it isn't necessary or wise to reveal your shortcomings, failings, illness, flaws, or story in the very early stages of a relationship—as it matures, it is vital to share these things. Eventually, they could impact your partner's life, and it is only fair that you fess up if you feel the relationship is going to the next level.

Know When to Run: 40 Ways to Tell He or She Is Not "The One"

1. Early on, he or she wants to know your personal data: how much money you

have, what your schedule is, name of your kids' schools, where you bank, and so on.

2. The person is perpetually late, stands you up, doesn't value your time.

3. He or she smothers you, almost stalks you.

4. There are too many secrets. It's been six months and you still haven't met his or her family or friends.

5. You are constantly fighting or arguing.

6. The person is always asking for money, help.

7. You have a nagging in your gut. You have a sense that something isn't right.

8. The person is married, going through a divorce, living with someone, or is in a relationship.

9. He or she courts you very quickly, pressures commitment or marriage.

10. You are criticized, even for petty things.

11. You are the brunt of his/her jokes, and if you protest, the response is: "Oh, you have no sense of humor!"

12. The person exhibits controlling behavior.

13. The person asks you for money, promising to repay when the ship comes in.

14. The person asks you to trust him or her with your money.

15. There is a lot of sexual innuendo.

16. You notice an obvious fetish or deviant nature.

17. The person treats you in a demeaning way.

18. He or she insists on monopolizing or manipulating your time.

19. You are discouraged from telling people you know about your new love interest.

20. There is unwarranted possessiveness or jealousy.

21. The person is suspicious of you.

22. You sense an overly concerned, veiled caring attitude.

23. There is a lack of trust when you're away, with friends, family.

24. The person shifts blame; everything is your fault.

25. You are undermined in the relationship.

26. The person has unrealistic expectations.

27. His/her needs are paramount.

28. Alcohol or substance abuse is evident.

29. The person is hypersensitive.

30. You are in danger of physical violence, abuse, verbal abuse, and emotional abuse.

31. You feel pressured to do things you normally would not do.

32. You do not share the same spiritual values.

33. He/she does not have a job, means of income, future goals.

34. He/she has a roommate of the same sex—and it's not an elderly relative who needs assistance.

35. The person does not have custody of, or see, his or her children.

36. The person belongs to a gang.

37. He/she sports tattoos with the names of old lovers.

38. The person has appeared on *The Bachelor*, *The Bachelorette*, or *Big Brother*.

39. The person hates chocolate.

40. _____. Go ahead. It's your turn. Fill in the blank.

When in Doubt, Check Him or Her Out!

Some people have a problem with this—you know, the right to privacy and all that, but I don't for one second want to subject my family or myself to danger; and at the very least, I do a Google and a Facebook search of anyone who will be in our lives: friends, caregivers, coaches, and dates. It can't hurt! If you have the dough-re-mi to cough up for more extensive paid searches, by all means, go for it. Definitely go for it—borrow if you have to—if you sense anything not right, or if you can't find anything about the person on the " 'net (which is rare, unless you are dating someone who does not use a computer or hand-held Internet-capable telephone).

The more information you have about the person before you go on the date, the better. Full Christian name and any nicknames, maiden names, friends' names, relatives' names, ex-spouse's name, are a good start. Date and place of birth, names of high school and college, grad year, current and past employment are also helpful.

Searches

Internet search engines such as google.com or yahoo.com, or free people search and publication information search engines such as zabasearch.com, pipl.com, or peekyou.com are useful. Check out also Facebook, Twitter, MySpace, genealogy sites, online police blotters, dating sites (many offer a free trial membership), or sites such as peoplefinders.com, reunion.com, or classmates.com, which, though free to search names, usually require a fee or upgrade for delivering more detailed results to you.

For a fee, some online companies perform background checks, criminal record searches, reverse phone and cell phone look-ups, and a variety of other public data searches, and will usually come up in your search engine results.

Precautionary Absolutes, Measures, and Boundaries

I never left my son alone with a boyfriend. There's just no need to ever leave a date alone with the children, unless you've known each other at least a year, and only then if you are in a committed relationship together, with marriage on the horizon and no hesitations at all. Even an inkling of mistrust for either your own or your child's safety should be immediate grounds to break off the relationship. You may deem this harsh or over the top, but today we can never be too careful when it comes to our children's safety. Child molesters, predators, kidnappers, and abusers can be male or female, and often are people we know, or people who seem too good to be true.

It is our responsibility to implement absolutes, measures, and boundaries to ensure the worst does not happen and to help us determine if someone can truly, unequivocally be trusted with our children. If you see or even sense any of the following behaviors—and by no means is this common-sense list complete—don't take any chances. Stop the misbehavior short, then immediately assess it, and take quick appropriate action to sever the relationship or call in the authorities to assist. I also urge you to do your own research. Knowledge is power. I do have a more comprehensive list in *The Single Parent's Guide to Raising Godly Children*.[4]

- The person seems very intent on spending time alone with your child, even manipulating events in order to babysit, take the child to the doctor, or pick up or take the child to school. He or she is always "conveniently" handy.

- The person seems intent to become your child's best friend.

- The person instructs or encourages your child to keep secrets or surprises from you.

- The person is too touchy-feely, or engages in too much physical play, tickling, tumbling, wrestling, and so on.

- The person wants to bathe the child, lay with the child while she goes to sleep.

- The person initiates private contact with your child by phone, text, e-mail, or on the Internet, or by chance meetings in the mall, outside the school, at playgrounds, sports fields, and so on.

- The person has a bad temper, is verbally, physically, or emotionally abusive. He or she teases too much, berates.

- The person uses sexual/suggestive language in the presence of the child, or directly targeted at the child.

Not settling is a practice and a promise. To further cement the deal to yourself, you might want to write out a pledge of allegiance and commitment to your family, and to yourself:

> I promise not to settle for someone less than the very best for me and my child. To be uncompromising in my beliefs and tried, tested, and true core values. To be honest about my feelings and motivations, determined to speak, seek, and uncover the truth for the benefit of those I love, and to respect myself and my family so deeply that I am even willing to remain single if I cannot find the right partner/ father (or mother) for us.
>
> Signature: _____
>
> Date: _____ / _____ / _____

Shae's "You Know What Ya Gotta Do" Chocolate-Covered Almonds Recipe

Yield: Lots

- 1 pound raw almonds, with skins on
- 1 cup water
- 2 cups granulated white sugar

- 12 oz. semisweet chocolate chips
- 2 cups icing (confectioner's) sugar OR 1 cup unsweetened cocoa

Combine the nuts, water, and granulated white sugar in a large heavy saucepan, bringing the mixture to a boil over a high heat. Maintain it just at a boil by adjusting the heat, stirring constantly until the syrup is completely reduced, the water evaporated and forming a sugar textured sandlike coating on the almonds; about 20 minutes. Keep your eye on it, you don't want the nuts to burn (or maybe you do!). Remove the pan completely from the heat. Spread the now-sugared almonds onto a parchment paper lined baking sheet, and place in the refrigerator until cool. In the meantime, place the semisweet chocolate in the top of a double boiler and gently melt to 88 degrees Fahrenheit. If the almonds are cool, break off excess clumps of sugar from them, and place half of the almonds in a large mixing bowl. Pour half of the melted chocolate into the bowl, stirring to fully coat, separate, and cool the almonds. Place the now chocolate covered nuts on a baking sheet lined with wax or parchment paper, and set aside. Place the remaining almonds in the chocolate, and repeat. Return the first batch of almonds to the mixing bowl, and pour in half of the icing sugar or cocoa into the bowl; stir until the almonds are coated and separated. Repeat with the remaining almonds until all have been fully coated. Store in a covered container in a cool place or in the freezer.

Calories: tons, but good fiber source, too!

Below the Surface

Date: _____

Are my children OK?

_____
_____
_____

What are their fears?

_____
_____
_____

What do they need?

_____
_____
_____

Who or what is my ultimate concern right now?

_____
_____

What has happened to me?

What is happening to me?

What's next?

What do I really want?

Why am I worried?

What am I most afraid of?

___

___

What is deep down inside of me that I haven't brought forth yet?

___

___

___

What do I have to offer?

___

___

___

What truths or lies have shaped my perceptions of me?

___

___

___

How faithful am I to my yearnings?

___

___

___

What sacrifices have I made?

___

___

___

Who has sacrificed for me?

What am I grateful for?

Who can I reach out to?

Who is the top person in my support network?

Who do I need to forgive?

What's the nut count?

Endnotes

1. Jason Jordan, quoted at http://www.lovequotescollection.com/quotes/jason_jordan.html.
2. *Misandrist* (archaic) meaning man hater, *misogynist* meaning woman hater, *misanthrope* meaning hater of people in general.
3. Author unknown.
4. *The Single Parent's Guide to Raising Godly Children* (Shippensburg, PA: Destiny Image, 2010).

Chapter Nine

Honey, I've Got Your Number

How to Break Up or Make Up Well

How to break up well. Now that sounds like an oxymoron, doesn't it? Breaking up was something I hated doing; as much if not more than I disliked firing an employee when I had my shop. Inevitably, though, breaking up with someone you've been dating will hurt to a degree one or both of you, and definitely the children are casualties of the loss, too, through no fault of their own. It is important, as you go through the process of a breakup or makeup, that your child's best interests and emotional health are kept at the forefront of your decisions.[1]

Breaking Up

The longer you've dated, perhaps the more painful breakup will be for all involved, including extended family members and close friends. It is easier said than done at times but the alternatives can be much more painful and harmful. Imagine your life a few years from now, or beyond. What would things be like then? I so thank God I'm where I am now.

Breaking up with someone may hurt, but it is pain with a purpose, in the spirit of *only the extraordinary will do for my family,* and in the spirit of letting go of something wrong to birth the right in all lives involved. Emotions may flare but trust that if you are breaking up for the right reasons, peace will resurface in the knowledge that you have done the right thing.

It can be terrifying to confront the truth about a bad relationship, especially if you've been in it for very long. I remember thinking at one point in a breakup, "Was I really that desperate? How could I have missed the warts?" But that was good, since I had to search my heart if there was to be any resolve, and thus arrived at appropriate enough answers to help me do the deed. I discovered I was human; I loved the feeling of being in love. I made a mistake, misjudged, forgave myself for the mistake, forgave the other person, and grew wiser and more understanding because of it, and could again move ahead with my plans. The most important thing was not to subject DS or myself any longer to something that was unhealthy for both of us. It took courage, it took faith, and it took asking myself some difficult questions, before I could push the broom.

Five Reasons Why We Tend to Cling to a Sinking Ship

Many of us find it hard to break up when we should. We let things go a little too long, but holding on to someone who isn't right for us (or the reverse, you may not be right for the other) is like holding on to a mistake, and the "mistake" becomes a ball and chain, dragging, slowing, and distracting us, perhaps even negatively affecting our emotional or physical health, how well we do our jobs, our outlook, our self-esteem, our responsibilities, all which will affect at some point the well-being of the children.

Some of you out there have been dating the same person for years and years. You might want to commit, but he or she hedges, doesn't seem ready, isn't willing to leap in faith. You might even be engaged but with no date on the horizon. I know of a couple who have been engaged for 23 years! It's time to break up and move on before you regret lost prime-time years. The truth is, some people never settle down, can't see themselves forever together in monogamy. You might be that person who is afraid of commitment.

1. *We tend to rationalize misbehavior,* especially if infatuated with the person or he or she has a good relationship with the children (see previous chapter). Some of us rationalize because of one or two outstanding qualities, perhaps those on your bonus list. We might also rationalize the time already invested, but time is never wasted on an incompatible partner because we grow and learn by experience. Every "wrong" relationship gets us a step or more closer to the right one.

2. *We just don't have the energy to go fishing again.* We don't want to go through the profiles, sift through the junk, place another ad, go to another social, endure another testing period, suffer more rejection, lose another arm or leg....Letting go of the "mistake," relieving yourself of your bondage to this person, breaking this unhealthy tie will in time reenergize you.

3. *We haven't dealt with the fear of being single or alone.* We are not comfortable or secure enough in ourselves (see Chapter Four).

4. *Because without us, the person will stumble, fumble, or crumble.* Maybe you think he's serious when he says he'll kill himself, or maybe you don't want to hurt her. She's weak; she won't survive. Although wanting not to hurt or desiring to save a person is honorable, our primary responsibility is to take care of our children's needs; and that's where we need to be playing the role of superman or wonder woman, saving our children. Understand, you are not responsible for this person's happiness, life, or choices. Indeed, assess the situation, and if she takes too much time away from you helping your own family, if he needs professional

help, in the absence of his own loved ones who can arrange it, direct him or her to it. If the person threatens suicide, call the authorities or a family member.

5. *Because we're afraid of making a mistake* in a "you don't know what you've got 'til it's gone" manner. If you're incompatible now, you will be incompatible, perhaps even more so, in the future. Face the fact that you are holding on to the wrong person, and do something about it. Rather than force yourselves together, free each other to find your respective "perfect for you" partners. If you don't want a future wedding ring to look like miniature handcuffs, develop a plan now to connect with yourself, thoroughly examining your core beliefs, and determining in advance that if a love interest does not share them, you will move on.

 CATCH THE DRIFT: Hurtful people can create an opportunity for love, not despair. The best thing we can do for those who persecute us is to love them as human beings and pray for them.[2]

I'm sure there are more than 50 ways to leave your lover, as Paul Simon's 1970s song goes, but there are a few "must-do" basics before you do.

Don't tell your children before the fact. Some might disagree with this, but if this person has been in your life for any length, and he or she and your children have met, don't tell them about it until you are done with the breaking up. Children don't need to get into our problems. Understand though, and be prepared to offer counsel to your children if you anticipate their grieving the loss.

List the reasons why beforehand. If you have invested any amount of time with a person, likely there was a whole lot of emotion there, too, which can make leaving more difficult. Writing down why you are leaving will help you remember why when emotions run high, or if your partner tries to convince you otherwise, or to help you keep to the facts.

Make a plan. Plan the logistics of separation ahead of time. If he or she has a key to your home, either change the locks or ask for the key back. Plan for back-up, supportive friends or family members, in case things get heated. Call the police if you are afraid of violence. Don't confront at home, especially not in front of the children.

Speak person-to-person. Forget the "Dear John or Jane" e-mail, voicemail, text, or Facebook or MySpace message; get in his or her space, unless that person has been abusive in some way. Face-to-face good-byes are about respecting the other person enough to explain; this, in turn, might just help him or her in future relationships.

Select the best time, best place. I had a high school boyfriend break up with me once on the eve of my graduation. Don't break up on Christmas or New Year's Eve, on a birthday, or at a family funeral, for goodness' sake!

Determine the best time and place by figuring out the worst, and by all means, do it in private, since emotions may run high.

Tell the truth. Avoid criticizing, accusing, and fault finding, toward your date or yourself. Stick to the root of the reason. It's much better to say, "We don't share the same dreams," than it is to say, "You are a lazy bum." Tell the truth with honey, pointing out his strengths, what you do like about him, and what did work. Be specific about what didn't work, and take responsibility for your part, also explaining why you are choosing not to work toward making things better. Avoid the standard, unauthentic break-up lines that, while gentler-sounding in delivery, are received like a mail bomb. Avoid especially, "It's not you…it's me," or, "I want to do this before you get too attached to me, so look at it as if I'm doing you a favor."

Don't blame yourself for wanting out. You have good reasons for saying good-bye, especially so as a single parent with so much to consider; thus, likely it does not mean you are being selfish or wrong in your decision. Don't let him or her guilt you into staying in the relationship for the wrong reasons.

Be empathetic. Recognize how difficult ending a love relationship is for both parties. "I know what it feels like when someone breaks up with me, and my heart goes out to you, but it's not good for either of us if we let this go further." Or, "I understand that you're hurt; it's not the way I'd hoped things would turn out. Please forgive me for hurting you; it was not my intention."

Steer it if possible to mutual agreement. Give the person a chance to respond, to share his or her emotions and feelings with you, but don't put yourself in danger or accept insult. Once the initial shock wears off and emotions wind down, he or she may want to talk about things more, which is all good toward to the letting-go stage.

Claim your boundaries. Make it a clean break and insist the person not contact you or your children—ever again, if you feel it would emotionally harm your children or you, or for a set period. This also gives you the space you and your children need to heal, regroup, recover, and move on.

Avoid rebound relationships. I read somewhere that particularly with men, the deeper the hurt the quicker the attachment to someone new. This might be because women are more likely to have and seek solace from a social support network, while a man tends to suck it up, hold it in, walk it off, in the more traditional masculine sense. If you are a single poppa, understand that while flying into the arms of someone might for a time buck you back up again, restore your manhood, help you control or release some emotions, these will likely bring a false sense of comfort. Rebound relationships are usually based on need and have a greater chance of failing; thus, it is better to avoid them, give yourself space, and seek a proper support network.

Making Up After a Break Up

> "Absence sharpens love, presence strengthens it."
>
> —ENGLISH PROVERB

Have you separated or broken up with someone whom you've discovered you still love very much? Whether you are planning to get back with your spouse or have decided to give a dating relationship another go, be sure you've given yourself enough time to assess if indeed it is workable or salvageable. Sometimes your separation has created enough space to ease the tension of your partnership enough to see if reconciliation is possible. Have you given yourself enough time to think about the problems that were in your relationship, how you feel, and about the realities of getting back together? If you are truly hoping to rebuild or rekindle a relationship, it is important to keep communication open and honest as you sort things out. It's not right and downright unfair to hold back, no matter how scared you are of rejection, or how many wrongs you did in the original relationship. If you'll recall, with Phil, we both held back our feelings. The relationship did have potential for reconciliation, but not without communicating even the basic, "I still love you, want you, miss you."

There does have to be a balance, while apart of working things out together while still finding time to grow stronger and more decisive about the situation, and about what is best for you and your family. It might be helpful to seek a counselor or therapist, pastor or rabbi, who might be able to help you see things that you cannot see, help maximize the effectiveness of your communication, or help you forgive any wrongdoings.

You also have to consider the possibility of handling an issue of infidelity or a rebound involvement during your time of separation, and this can be quite hard for one or both parties to accept, not to mention, in light of a sexual affair, the possibility of sexually transmitted diseases. Being apart for any substantial length increases the amount of stuff you'll have to work through in the making up process.

Separation may have indeed helped you realize how much you value each other. Moreover, with firmer resolve to renew your desires to strengthen the relationship, to really work at making it healthy. If reconciling, ensure you both make a sincere commitment to doing this, even going as far as making new vows to each other, and this can be done whether married or not.

Be attentive to signs that the other party is just as keen to reconcile as you are. If you are unsure or not convinced, don't make up just yet. It could be that the make-up attempts have resurrected old hurts or anger that he or she still has to work through.

There is hope that your relationship can re-blossom stronger and healthier than ever before, but you have to fix the mistakes and problems that led to the separation in the first place, and ensure they stay fixed.

Determine the root cause/s. For instance, your partner may have had an affair. Your inattentiveness and/or his insecurity in your love may be the underlying reasons why. Almost every symptom has a root, something driving it. If you cannot find it, perhaps you or your partner's emotions are still too raw to see beyond the surface. Unless you do, though, similar issues will arise, perhaps manifesting differently, but ultimately because of the same root problem.

Fix the cause/s. To fix the cause takes you both working through it, and together. But you're almost there, having discovered it! What can you do to make him feel more loved? Can you be more attentive? Can you stop giving him the silent treatment? And can he commit to communicating his feelings better? Here we see again a mutual and balanced give-and-take process.

Rebuild your relationship from the first-blush stage up, as if it is something entirely new—because, in effect, it is. Court each other, date each other as if you've just met. Get to know each other again, but this time being aware of the inevitable and necessary stages toward a healthy relationship.

Plan your future. If you both have something to work toward together, you will feel more empowered to reach greatness in your relationship. Along the way, find something new that you can do as a couple, take up a hobby, a sport, something that creates opportunity to be together and that will create opportunity by being together.

Resolve to stop blame and grant pardon. Drop the burdens of the past, and you will gain wonderful harvest as a result.

Below the Surface

Date: _____

Are my children OK?

_____
_____
_____

What are their fears?

What do they need?

Who or what is my ultimate concern right now?

What has happened to me?

What is happening to me?

What's next?

What do I really want?

Why am I worried?

What am I most afraid of?

What is deep down inside of me that I haven't brought forth yet?

What do I have to offer?

What truths or lies have shaped my perceptions of me?
_____
_____
_____

How faithful am I to my yearnings?
_____
_____
_____

What sacrifices have I made?
_____
_____
_____

Who has sacrificed for me?
_____
_____
_____

What am I grateful for?
_____
_____
_____

Who can I reach out to?
_____
_____
_____

Who is the top person in my support network?

Who do I need to forgive?

Endnotes

1. *The Single Parent's Guide to Raising Godly Children* (Shippensburg, PA: Destiny Image, 2010).
2. This interesting perspective of justice and love is from the words of Jesus Christ, found in the New Testament of the Holy Bible, Book of Matthew, Chapter 5, verses 43-48. A good cross-reference is the Book of Ecclesiastes, found in the Old Testament, Chapter 3, verses 16-20.

Chapter Ten

Try Again, Draw a Long Breath, and Believe

Take Your Relationship to Extraordinary Heights

> *"I can't believe that!" said Alice.*
>
> *"Can't you?" the queen said, in a pitying tone. "Try again, draw a long breath, and shut your eyes."*
>
> *Alice laughed. "There's no use trying," she said. "One can't believe impossible things."*
>
> *"I dare say you haven't had much practice," said the queen. "When I was your age, I always did it for half an hour a day. Why, sometimes I've believed as many as six impossible things before breakfast."*[1]

Do you ever wonder why, in fairytales, the end of the story happens when the prince and princess finally meet "and they lived happily ever after." What's with that? In real life, they were in relationship stage one, the beginning of their story: the attraction phase, where all similarities are apparent and celebrated (oh my gosh, *you* wear shoes, too?), and it's like, "Welcome to Fantasy Island." They're all over each other, each has found his/her One And Only: in him, her brawny cut knight, in her, his fair maiden, and all the two can "see" is their riding off on a white horse into the sunset of euphoric bliss. Although the Cinderella/fella fantasy is admirable, fine, and sweet, it takes more than a dream or feelings to make a relationship work and keep it from going into Once Upon A Time mode.

> **Most healthy relationships don't just happen with a flick of a wand, the stroke of a clock, or the wiggle of a nose.**

Most healthy relationships don't just happen with a flick of a wand, the stroke of a clock, or the wiggle of a nose; they take months, sometimes a few years, to develop. They may require flexibility, endurance, perseverance, courage, humor, and a willingness by both to wait and work through inevitable and necessary challenges and stages before commitment, even breaking it off if necessary. Particularly so the single parent with children at home, who are affected by their parent's relationships. If you want your relationship to grow from headlock to wedlock, read on.

Relationship Stages

"Chicken Little" Stage

All relationships need to go through stages, which is why we shouldn't rush into marriage. Stage one naturally wears off, and everyone will progress to Stage Two, the Chicken Little phase, which happens after you've known each other for a while. This is where the sky falls either a little or a lot. You think that real life is just about to begin but discover a potential obstacle, something to be dealt with, before life can begin. You bring a little more of yourself into the scene; he brings some baggage, but because the blush hasn't worn off, one or both of you may still head for the sunset.

"Cluck-Cluck" Stage

At this point, we should brush off the blush and move into the Cluck-Cluck stage, PDQ, to determine if the sky actually might be falling. Can Princess really live with Prince's flaw? Prince with her quirk? Their differences? Because in marriage the tiniest annoyance can magnify a thousand-fold. Is it an intrinsic quirk, like a weird laugh? If so, put it under your imaginary super zoom magnifying glass and imagine living forever with it.

I dated the most wonderful fellow, the most perfect spousal candidate I could imagine, handsome as all get out, an ex-football player, wonderful father, who loved children and animals, was extremely romantic and attentive, and had a good and secure job. Everything about him was stellar, except for one thing. His laugh, which sounded like a moose impersonating Eddie Murphy. I handled it on the first few dates—I mean, he was gorgeous. By date five, however, I would have traded that quirk in for an extra 300 pounds on his perfect body or a fingernails-on-chalkboard fetish. I tried avoiding comedy, told the saddest stories. Still he laughed. Happy by nature, everything amused him. He was the kind of person who could burst out laughing in the middle of a dead silence because of something that happened the previous year. Normally, a sense of humor in a man is attractive, but sincerely, people weren't staring and pointing at him in restaurants because he was a hunk. I did everything I could to change it, even googling "Can a person change his laugh?" and "How to tell someone you love that you hate his laugh, without hurting his feelings." By and by, however, he broke up with me, likely not impressed with my Eeyore-like sad behavior!

Many such quirks are not necessarily grounds for breakup. To your ears it might sound like the mating call of a moose and something you'd be content with for the rest of your life. Or his laugh might make you giggle. Conversely, it might be your quirk that breaks a deal. Everyone has at least one. For instance, my snoring can wake the dead. This might not bother a deep sleeper. Or, you might like to drench all of your food with catsup, and this might not even raise a *tsk tsk* on a date. But again, every quirk should be put under a lens because it might just be a symptom of an underlying problem, although when it comes to catsup, I can't think what that might be.

I remember, early on in one relationship, thinking how "boy-like" a certain person was in the way he never picked up for himself. It endeared me to him, and I could imagine myself taking care of this boy man and finally organizing his life for him. In commitment, this became a huge issue though, and hear me, I am not a neat freak and have always concurred with my mother's credo, "My house is clean enough to be healthy, and messy enough to be comfortable." But this fellow, oh my goodness, the cuteness wore off when I had to live with it. This endearing "flaw" was, in actuality, a symptom of deeper challenges of sloppiness, procrastination, and laziness.

> "My house is clean enough to be healthy, and messy enough to be comfortable."

I share this with you not to condemn him but, by golly, I'd put a bundle of folded laundry on a stair for the next person to take up, and this two-hundred-pound strong man would go out of his way to step over it. The only chore he would agree to was to take out the garbage once a week the night before, but he seldom did it. He rarely awoke before early afternoon, putting in only an hour or two of work, usually by phone, although his outside sales job required him and paid him to be in his territory at least eight hours a day. He'd empty the contents of his electric shaver all over the countertop and floor and leave it, rub food spills into the carpet with his shoe, wouldn't change his clothes or socks for a week, and horror, he'd floss his teeth at the dinner table and let it fly. Although I had a business and worked 12-plus-hour days, I also, along with the housework, had to do most of the yard work and home maintenance to boot.

This at first appeared as a small quirk. Imagine seeing a *significant* flaw right from the start and how humongous it could become. Alcoholism, having a quick temper, coldness or distance, being into porn, or being stuck up or noncommittal. These are things we have to honestly preassess. If it is small, does it have potential to loom larger? Is it a portent of a greater challenge? Something we can handle? It might help by going back to the deal breaker "I'm Outta Here" list we created in Chapter Eight.

"Give and Take" Stage

If the flaws aren't deal breakers, you enter into the mutual Give-and-Take stage immediately. Say he doesn't want you to work but you want to continue your career. You talk, listen to concerns, rationally think things through, both give a little, take a little, sacrifice a little, to come to a mutually acceptable compromise, even a pact. Love *and* using your head before commitment is vital if the relationship is to flourish. Do it now, since once you are in a marriage, you may have to compromise a whole lot more: "Look, you promise to grow up, pick up after yourself, switch to a straight razor, floss in the bathroom, shampoo the carpet, and I'll overlook the socks, get a boob job, and wear that hot little spaghetti strap number you love so much, more often."

"Easy Does It" Stage

The next stage is the Easy Does It stage, with the *i do take thee* stage, to follow. In both of these stages you still have to use your head and abide by the give-and-take law because you'll be going through more challenges, friction, or struggle: In going steady, introducing the children and families and finding more time together. In marriage, with the full reality of a new family. Before marriage is the time to ensure the relationship is on an even slope, not leaning to one side but balanced. Meaning, you are not the one doing all the giving, or the taking! If you are the only one giving in the relationship, stop. Save that extra energy for your children, who will benefit more from it. This kind of relationship lean-to is not healthy at all, and eventually will grow resentment or bitterness in your heart toward your "taking" partner. Interestingly, many single parents lean toward the taking part in a romantic relationship because they give so much of themselves into their families and survival, and so much has been taken from them or lost. This was the case for me in more than one instance after my marriage breakup. Understandably, my love interest at the time, who also had children of his own, eventually, for his own and his family's well-being, had to stop giving so much of himself to me, and I didn't handle the sudden 180 well! Find a healthy balance! Stay within even boundaries, maintaining a strong sense of self-esteem, and family identity. Ensure a reasonable exchange. Totally immersing yourself into your partner such that you lose your individuality may doom the relationship.

Are your children OK? Continue to check in on them!

Become an amazing listener. I tend to stop communicating when I try to share my heart or concerns with a person but that person won't listen. I think it's natural for all of us. Listening to your partner without judging, putting off, thinking about something else, interjecting, or discounting will make him or her feel understood, respected, valued, cherished, adored, and loved. If your honey has clammed up, it could be an inward struggle to resist you. Remember Kermit and Piggy's relationship? He wanted to resist her, would not commit, but let some handsome male costar even breathe her name with a sultry tone and he'd let him have it. He loved her—he just couldn't say, "I love you." There are tons of resources out there on how to become a more effective communicator.

Tiptoe through some tulips: Laugh and play. Unless you have a moose laugh, laugh a lot. Happy, humorous people, to me, are the most attractive. Laughter can deepen or create a bond that buffers even the greatest disappointments, defusing conflict and acting as a pressure relief valve. Hanging on to humor, especially after the blush wears off, may rescue your relationship from the doldrums. Play will create laughter, and is a great tool for keeping things vital, alive, and fresh in relationship, giving it some zip, lightening the heavies, and heightening the sense of intimacy and connection. If you've had a disagreement, mutual laughter may bring you back together, neutralizing the situation. Be careful, though. Don't use humor as a cover-up to how you feel, or to tease, ridicule, or cover up the truth because this breeds mistrust. If your partner is not enjoying it, stop and back off. This was a huge problem in one of my relationships. The teasing really hurt, and eventually created a deep unbridgeable chasm. If you have offended, immediately apologize. Using humor to interrupt an argument may give both of you a chance to reconnect, or regain perspective, by easing the tension.

This in itself may even shake you free of rigid thinking to help you find a creative solution or compromise. It reduces defense mechanisms as well as inhibitions. If you haven't at least giggled or guffawed in a while, you might need practice. Play with your children or frolic with a puppy, bunny, or kitten. Watch or read cartoons, ballroom dance in your living room with a broom, audition for *American Idol* in the shower, imagine Simon's response, watch some silly pet tricks on YouTube, recall happier times. The more you practice, the more spontaneous laughter becomes. If by a teeny-weeny chance you discover your laugh is like that of a hyena (or a moose), you may want to pick up a canned laughter tape, or place a call to the North Pole for a lesson in Ho! Ho! Ho!

Tune in to his or her deeper needs, and cherish and steward them well. Again, this is part of communicating, asking questions, delving deeply into your partner's heart—its motivations, its history, its hurts, its longings, its dreams. But be careful with the knowledge. Never trash his needs. Don't discard them. Don't use them as tools of revenge or anger or accusation or control. Ouch, I can think of several times when something I've shared in confidence has been thrown in my face to hurt me. Knowing this stuff should help you avoid misreading a motive or need of the heart, or overreacting, and as a result, get into relationship-breaking arguments. Use what you know to be proactive, helpful, understanding, mindful, careful, protective, nurturing, fulfilling, and strengthening. This is the deepest form of respect.

Focus on what your relationship needs. Does it need better communication? More spice? More honesty? Less criticism?

More time together? Less time together? More play? Children more included? Forgiveness? Apology? Contrary to the popular belief that love means never having to say you are sorry, true love does require repentance for wrongdoings. True love is humble. True love forgives. True love does not lash out. True love is not prideful. Yes, think things through using your head—but with your heart, always choose to forgive, to reconcile.

Decide that you will be an extraordinary girlfriend, boyfriend, or life partner. This is particularly hard for the single parent already with so much to focus on, but being extraordinary in relationship is not about giving your everything but about giving your best. The best of you. Mediocrity only takes a relationship so far, it's not enough to carry it when things get rough, to sustain satisfaction in it. An extraordinary lover does things that a mediocre one likely will not; goes out of his or her way to make things right, to grow the relationship, to give, to nurture, to steward it. Mediocre runs dry, may give up, may react. Extraordinary replenishes the flow of unconditional love, showers the respect, turns on the passion and compassion. And, extraordinary will breed extraordinary results, feedback, and reciprocal super-duper, creating the relationship of your dreams. It's powerful! William James said: "To change one's life: Start immediately. Do it flamboyantly. No exceptions."[2]

Decide today that you will be an extraordinary and flamboyant partner.

Discover ways in which to deal with and settle disagreements that draw you closer. Closer, rather than creating a gulf.

This might involve listening and tuning in, resolving that you never part angry with one another or never have to have the last word on a matter. It might be that you promise yourself to count to a hundred before a retort, to "sit" on a cell phone text or e-mail or letter for a few days before sending it to ensure your words aren't lashing out, belittling, accusatory, reactive. It might be that you raise the white flag even if you are convinced you are right and he or she is wrong. Truth eventually surfaces. It might be better to retreat. Is there a better, more nurturing way of getting your point across? Make sure you fight fair. Don't attack. Don't drag old arguments in. Keep the focus in the immediate issue. Respect your partner. And, if you feel the urge to throw something, make sure it is chocolate, since it's probably going to be tossed back![3] Yum! Yum!

Let some things slide. Benjamin Franklin, himself a person with strong core values and success in marriage, said, "Keep your eyes wide open before the wedding, half shut afterwards."[4] In other words, as long as your significant other is trying his or her best most of the time, let the other 10 or 20 percent slide (unless it's abusive). Don't lash out, unglue, clam up, belittle, criticize. It's not healthy to call someone on every little mistake. Indeed, if this person shares your hopefully exemplary values, there is little more worth fussing about and less worry that your relationship will become a three-ring circus event: engagement ring, wedding ring, and suffering!

Stop trying to be right all the time. This will take much pressure off of you and speaks for itself! Although it is admirable to have strong convictions, you'll find the greater traits are in giving people opportunity to be heard, and in being open to changing your own opinion, raising a white flag, in favor of exposure of the truth or fact. Of course, I could be wrong....

Discover different ways to ignite, reignite, or grow the passion between you. Check the balance. Are you more friends than lovers? Lovers than friends? Two strangers? Nourish the love, Baby! You know how....

Focus on your partner's good qualities. Especially when my relationships were in a rut, I was more apt to point out or see my partner's flaws, and vice versa. In a few cases, the flaws outweighed the positives and were hard to ignore. However, if someone's core values, standards, and qualities are generally positive, focus there. This will create an ever-growing strength in your relationship, and reduce resentment or bitterness.

Expect the ups and downs. Circumstances change, losses happen, and you won't always be on the same page with someone. Different people cope and react differently. Realizing this and extending grace is paramount to getting through the rough stuff. Avoid taking your problems out on your honey, even if you feel a release in doing so because it will slowly poison the relationship. Consider couples or marriage counseling or individual help if the problem is bigger than both of you. Or check in with your pastor, rabbi, or spiritual advisor.

Understand the most important needs of a single parent woman in relationship. First, of course, that I not only find the right person for me but for my son as well. Important to me (and to many surveyed single-parent women), is to be in relationship with a man who is willing to pick up the heavier suitcases of life, who will carry the emotional, physical, spiritual crosses, stand in the gap, be the yoke. I desire a man who will be the pastor and caretaker of not only my own, but my child's heart as well, without question, hesitation, or tarrying. Someone who will not only open car doors but the figurative doors of my heart, freeing me to love, freeing me to live, freeing my femininity, freeing the woman in me. Someone who will help me protect my child, and nurture and steward the child within him. Someone who doesn't pick up the grocery bag of bread and hand me the bag with the four liters of milk for the mile-walk home, if you know what I mean. Someone who really does get under my skin to feel my true feminine make-up. I want to be made to feel like a woman, to be a woman, because I am a woman, and I love being a woman. Someone who respects my devotion to motherhood. Particularly, I don't want to be compared to anyone else, even if it is Marilyn Monroe or Mother Teresa, because I want to be special to someone for who I am. I need to know for sure that a person is there for us no matter what looking out for our best interest, protecting our physical, emotional, and spiritual health, and never threatening us with abandonment. Chameleons need not apply.

Understand the most important needs of a single-parent man in relationship. Special thanks for the following insight from several savvy single-dating-parent dads. As with the SP moms, their greatest need is also to find the right fit for the family. Men, too, don't want changelings in their lives. "Be the same person I initially fell in love with." There appears to be greater levels of trepidation among SP dads that someone will drastically change in marriage for the worse, as in the wicked stepmother scenario. Single dads surveyed seem less likely to jump into remarriage, as a result of this fear of being duped. The slug syndrome—dressing down, letting oneself go, gaining too much weight, less attention on personal hygiene—is a similar concern. They don't want marriage transforming the woman into someone a man doesn't even recognize. Men desire frequent affection, physical contact, and spice. Touch goes a long way: hugs, handholding, signs that say: "I need you, love you, want you." Highly visual, it is important to a man that a woman does not stop caring for herself. Some men are worried that women are more interested in their potential, rather than in who they are or where they're at, viewing men more as projects. To paraphrase Mark Twain, women marry men hoping they will change while men marry women hoping they will not.[5] This is a recipe for disappointment, to be sure.

Read the love signs, transmit love signs. It is said that the heart seldom feels what the mouth expresses.[6] Some people, more so men, find it hard to describe or share their feelings. If you are finding it hard to read someone's feelings about you, look for signs. How does he react when he sees you? Do his eyes light up? Does he smile? If you bump into each other unexpectedly at the mall, is he happy to see you? How does she react when you discuss a future together? Does she blow it off, or does she dream with you? If your son jokingly calls him "Daddy 2," do you see terror in his eyes? Does she take or show interest in what interests you? Does she remember that you don't take sugar in your coffee? Your middle name?

Do you fit into his plans, or does he pencil you in? Will she tell you when you have parsley in your teeth? Does he laugh at your jokes? Is he making plans to be with you? Have you met the parents? Friends? Does he brush the dog hair off your coat for you? Has she discussed the future with you? Remember, he or she may be looking for similar signs from you, but don't smother, and don't cling!

Frequently restate your commitment to the person, to the relationship. Unconditional love is just that. I have a friend, Susan, who, every time she and her husband have an argument, either leaves or banishes him to the couch. Jim, a single divorced parent, shares that every time he and his ex went through a difficulty, she would threaten him with divorce, and it became a self-fulfilling prophecy. Although you never want to stay in an abusive relationship, when normal stuff happens—disagreements, small mistakes, and so on—threatening to leave, break it off, or divorce or telling the other person to leave as a means of "winning" the argument is not healthy, kind, or loving. If your child does something wrong, you don't automatically kick her out of the house or threaten to abandon her, do you? Hopefully not. If your partner's basic core values, standards, and qualities are positive, focus there. This will create an ever-growing strength in your relationship. It is much better to help one another gain confidence in each other such that you can both find rest and comfort in the safety of your future together.

Don't involve too many people in your relationship problems. Nobody knows you like you do. Nobody knows your partner like you do. Nobody knows what goes on like you do.

In constantly running to your mother, to your best friend, to her friends, his buddies, you are in danger of receiving an avalanche of wrong advice, of straying, of hard feelings, of pulling farther apart.

Keep up with your own interests, goals, life, dreams, and family. The last thing you want to do is live your life vicariously through someone else, without backbone of your own. Independence is sexy; intelligence is attractive. Without a life of your own, how can you share your life *with* another?

Avoid ultimatums or succumbing to one. Certainly many people have married as a result of shotgun weddings, threats of breakup, and the "If you don'ts, I won'ts." In general, though, few people respond well to such ultimatums—so don't twist arms or emotions to get what you want. I won't mention which relationship, but in one of them, I was coerced and made to fear what would happen if I did not commit to him. It is better for someone to make the choice to be with you and your children forever without coercion, or blackmail, to be with you because it is his or her choice to be with you and the little ones. If it comes by pressure, eventually you and your family may be seen as more of a burden than a blessing, inviting control or emotional or physical abuse of you and the children. If someone really loves and cherishes you and your children, do you think he or she would let you get away? Giving the person his or her freedom to choose to love you forever is like handing him or her a bottle of I'm-stuck-to-you-forever glue.

Don't undermine. A surefire way to create cold shoulders is to singe each other's intelligence, manhood, or womanhood. Even worse, in public.

Avoid the silent treatment.

22 Signs That He or She Is Ready for Commitment

1. Introduces you to family, friends, co-workers.
2. You keep in close touch with one another.
3. Shows interest in what's going on in your child's life, in your life.
4. Shares what is going on in his or her life.
5. Saving or making concrete plans for your future together: house hunting, for instance!
6. You share deeper feelings, more history.
7. Finds time for you and the children, is available.
8. Wants to share the holidays with you.
9. Has no reservations, no doubts, no hedging.
10. Suggests premarriage counseling.
11. Expresses love in words and actions.
12. Seriously talks about being together.

13. Starts acting like a husband, wife.
14. In conversation, pronoun goes from "me" to "we."
15. His or her plans include you.
16. You don't have to pry for information.
17. Goes the extra mile to discover/share your interests.
18. Readily asks your opinion, consults you and respects your decisions.
19. The gifts get personal.
20. He or she would marry you now if it were possible.
21. He's got a ring sizer in his pocket.
22. Engagement with a set date.

Below the Surface

Date: _____

Are my children OK?

_____
_____
_____
_____

What are their fears?
_____
_____
_____

What do they need?
_____
_____
_____

Who or what is my ultimate concern right now?
_____
_____
_____

What has happened to me?
_____
_____
_____

What is happening to me?
_____
_____
_____

What's next?
_____
_____
_____

What do I really want?

Why am I worried?

What am I most afraid of?

What is deep down inside of me that I haven't brought forth yet?

What do I have to offer?

What truths or lies have shaped my perceptions of me?

Try Again, Draw a Long Breath, and Believe

How faithful am I to my yearnings?

What sacrifices have I made?

Who has sacrificed for me?

What am I grateful for?

Who can I reach out to?

Who is the top person in my support network?
_____
_____
_____

Who do I need to forgive?
_____
_____
_____

Got a nut?
_____
_____
_____

Endnotes

1. Lewis Carroll, *Through the Looking Glass, and What Alice Found There* (New York: Thomas Y. Crowell & Co., 1893; multiple reprints), Chapter 5: "Wool and Water."
2. William James, quoted in www.quotegarden.com/carpe-diem.html.
3. Just kidding. Never resort to violence!
4. Ben Franklin, quoted at www.1-love-quotes.com/Famous_Wedding_Toasts.htm.
5. Mark Twain, quote.
6. Quote attributed to Jean Galoert de Campistron. Quoted at www.worldofquotes.com/topic/Speech/index/html.

Summary

Again it's time to say, and in the words of Carol Burnett, I'm so glad we've had this time together. Thank you for letting me get so up close and personal. I respect your space, I sincerely do! What a privilege that you have shared it with me because, Lord knows, we have so little of it to ourselves!

As a single parent, you are a member of the most precious and spectacular group of people on the planet, braving the toughest winters to see the greatest springs as you do. And I honor and applaud you for enduring and overcoming tough emotional odds to fend for your family, for protecting the innocence of our youth who really are our future, and for spreading so much wealth of love around even when you're spread so thin.

Perhaps you have noticed that we haven't covered the actual tying of the knot, and all that it entails in logistics concerning the blending of families and the starting of a new life. This may be included in a future issue of the *Single Parent's Guide* because the stats are cause for concern, and it's a complex subject, deserving of a book on its own. Many remarriages end in redivorce. Perhaps this is because people overlook the dynamics of a second marriage, which is so much different from a first marriage. If you're close to a commitment now, please research the subject, or seek counseling concerning it, because knowing and understanding those differences will help you prepare for and accept them into your new normal. Being aware will help you and your partner commit to doing it right.

I also urge you to gain a good support network. It is critical at this stage. And remember, troubles and challenges are a part of all of our lives. If we don't share them, we don't give those we love opportunity to love us enough.

Before we close, take a moment and examine your "Below the Surface" lists found at the end of each chapter, and the answers you've provided. Likely, your answers have not remained the same. This is a good sign! You've caught the drift! Use your answers as markers to gauge your growth and healing, and don't stop asking yourself questions, even if they are over the top.

I'm praying for unconditional love to pervade your life, sparking miracles.

Joy in Love,

Shae

PS: I welcome your response, opinions, questions, successes, or challenges, and invite you to write or e-mail:

Shae Cooke
PO Box 78006
Port Coquitlam, BC
Canada, V3B 7H5
E-mail: singleparentguide@gmail.com
Web site: www.shaecooke.com

About Shae Cooke

P.O. Box 78006
Port Coquitlam, BC
Canada, V3B 7H5
www.shaecooke.com
Main Email: shaesyc@telus.net
Email: singleparentguide@gmail.com
Alternates: powderpuffshae@gmail.com
shaesy2000@yahoo.com

In the Right Hands, This Book will Change Lives!

Most of the people who need this message will not be looking for this book. To change their lives, you need to put a copy of this book in their hands.

> *But others (seeds) fell into good ground, and brought forth fruit, some a hundred-fold, some sixty-fold, some thirty-fold* (Matthew 13:8).

Our ministry is constantly seeking methods to find the good ground, the people who need this anointed message to change their lives. Will you help us reach these people?

> *Remember this—a farmer who plants only a few seeds will get a small crop. But the one who plants generously will get a generous crop* (2 Corinthians 9:6).

**EXTEND THIS MINISTRY BY SOWING
3 BOOKS, 5 BOOKS, 10 BOOKS, OR MORE TODAY,
AND BECOME A LIFE CHANGER!**

Thank you,

Don Nori Sr., Publisher
Destiny Image
Since 1982

DESTINY IMAGE PUBLISHERS, INC.

"Speaking to the Purposes of God for This Generation and for the Generations to Come."

VISIT OUR NEW SITE HOME AT
WWW.DESTINYIMAGE.COM

FREE SUBSCRIPTION TO DI NEWSLETTER

Receive free unpublished articles by top DI authors, exclusive discounts, and free downloads from our best and newest books.
Visit www.destinyimage.com to subscribe.

Write to: Destiny Image
             P.O. Box 310
             Shippensburg, PA 17257-0310

Call: 1-800-722-6774

Email: orders@destinyimage.com

For a complete list of our titles or to place an order online, visit www.destinyimage.com.

FIND US ON FACEBOOK OR FOLLOW US ON TWITTER.

www.facebook.com/destinyimage
www.twitter.com/destinyimage